What Kids Need Most In A Dad

IF YOU WANT TO BE A BETTER DAD,

But you realize there are no easy answers . . .

If you want to rediscover
the joy of being a dad and some of the hard work
that goes along with it . . .

If you're interested in some positive,
biblical philosophy on being a father and want
some solid suggestions and practical insights
from a dad who struggles, too . . .

READ THIS BOOK!

What Kids Need Most In A Dad

Tim Hansel

Fleming H. Revell Company
Old Tappan, New Jersey

Library of Congress Cataloging in Publication Data

Hansel, Tim
    What kids need most in a dad.

    Bibliography: p.
    1. Fathers. 2. Parenting—Religious aspects—
Christianity. I. Title.
HQ756.H365   1984   646.7'8   83-22902
ISBN 0-8007-1390-7

This one's for you, Dad.
Thanks for teaching me, and showing me,
what it means to "Never Give Up."
♥

And to Steve, my "other dad."
No one ever had a brother like this.

Contents

Acknowledgments

This is a book that, in many ways, I didn't want to write. But for reasons which you'll soon find out, I did. It ended up being far more difficult than I ever imagined—mainly because it has forced me to take an honest look at myself as a father, as a man, and as a husband. I suppose, in some ways, I had to go through a period of being lost in order to be found again. As painful as it was, it was certainly worth it. Possibly, if this book is truly directed by the Spirit, which I trust it is, then you, too, would be encouraged to go through such a journey of rediscovery.

Most of all, I'm grateful to my wife, Pam. Her courage and tenacity to not give in on her own uniqueness amidst some very trying and difficult circumstances is evidence to me of her own incredible journey in Christ.

Writing this book has been more than just a task; it has been an arduous personal journey. Special gratitude is owed to some friends who were, at the same time, confronting and compassionate. Jim and Debbie Baker were willing to listen, to love, and to challenge me in ways that few friends do.

Doug and Elsie Land opened up their home, their lives, and their studio out behind their house at a critical time. This book would never have been finished without them.

Gary and Peg Low opened their hearts, in the midst of their own pain, to believe in me more than I could in myself. Any words that I will ever put into print will have their initials hidden on each page with invisible ink.

There are so many others that I am afraid of leaving someone out. I hope they will see themselves in these pages. Men like Jack Meyer, Orv Mestad, Wes Mudge, Jerry Hay, Stephen Gibbs, John McEntyre, Jim Dobson, D. Dean Givens, Howard Zatkin, and my dear friend and neighbor Jon Sapp have all taught me more about fathering than any books could.

We are all children as well as parents. Some day Zac and Josh (our boys) and Amber, Sven, and Christopher (our godchildren) will also understand the struggles and joys of being a parent. Thanks for being the "very particular kids" in our lives and for giving a daily substance to all these words.

And finally, my wholehearted thanks to Arline Hampton, whose magic fingers typed this manuscript with uncanny accuracy and speed, and to Fritz Ridenour for his friendship and invaluable editing.

Foreword

What Dads Need Most in a Book

To paraphrase an old saying, when God realized He couldn't be everywhere, He decided to make fathers.

This is a book about the dignity and struggle—and the fun—of being a dad. Moms might enjoy these thoughts, too. Their job is no less difficult or subtle. The reason this book is aimed primarily at dads, however, is twofold:

1. There aren't enough honest books for dads that admit to the intense strain and adventure of being a father.
2. I'm a dad. At the rate I'm going, I'll probably never be a mom. Therefore I can only speak with real integrity from a male parent's point of view.

I am deeply concerned about the future of the family and I think that the major breakdown is in the lives of those of us who call ourselves fathers. Being a dad is more than just being a male body that lives in the same house; it's more than just being a provider; it's even more than just being a good man.

No Easy Answers

My deepest hope is that these pages will stimulate you to reconsider your unique role as a husband and father. This book offers no easy answers, no magic formulas. In fact, the following words are being written during the most difficult, most painful period I've ever experienced. I hope that what I'm going through will serve to make this book more honest.

I was gravely tempted not to write it because of the difficulties, but I am slowly learning (again) that pain, difficulties, and disappointments are not to be avoided, because they lubricate our relationship with life at all levels.

John Donne, one of my favorite devotional writers, said it well: "Affliction is a treasure and scarce any man hath enough of it. No man hath affliction enough that is not matured and ripened by it and made for God by that affliction."

You will note that the title of this book is not *What Dads Want Most in Their Kids.* This is how too many dads tend to think. If only our kids were different, we could be better fathers. If only our kids would shape up, get better grades, be more squared away, be more like the neighbor kids, then things would be different. We could love them more, enjoy them more, accept them more. The title *What Kids Need Most in a Dad* is most appropriate. It reminds us that it is the fathers who must change and who must be renewed first. Other changes will follow.

I realize that many dads would simply prefer some new technique on "how to be a good dad" rather than genuine change and renewal. I can identify with that; I'm not crazy about changing, either. In my own fathering, I went for too long avoiding the real issues. But then I began to realize that I was missing the real point. I couldn't spend the rest of my life indefinitely "preparing to be a good dad." So, I made a decision. I would be the very best dad I could possibly be to my kids while I still had time. For the past several years, I have been doing that to the best of my abilities. I don't want this to be just a book "about fathering." I want it to be an honest book by an honest father who struggles, written to other honest fathers who struggle. As the writer of Proverbs said, "It is a wonderful heritage to have an honest father" (Proverbs 20:7 TLB).

Fathering Is Frequently Unpredictable

For me, being a father is more than just a good idea. It is an indelible fact, a reality full of intense joys and frustrations, hope and despair, great rewards and great failures. Fathering is unpredictable, untidy, and frequently confusing. I recently heard someone describe it like this: "I feel so often like I'm having an identity crisis and an energy crisis at the same time. I don't know who I am and I don't have the energy to find out."

Fathering can be like that in a lot of ways. I feel pushed and shoved in so many directions, it's sometimes hard for me to remember who I am and what I am here for.

But I am a father—a parent. *Father* is more than just a six-letter word. To be a father is a living reality that you and I participate in each day. The word *father* is so sacred that we even dare to describe God Himself with such a term. The word *father* is so difficult that in our lifetime we'll begin to discover only portions of its meaning. The word *father* is so powerful that what we do with it will affect the lives of our children forever.

So, I thank you in advance for struggling with me and for recognizing that the words on these pages are only meant to stimulate your thinking. As you read, I hope that you will have frequent occasion to put this book down and just go spend some time with your kids. These pages are only windows. I want you to look through them, of course, but above all, I want you to see, really *see,* your ultimate purpose as a parent.

We'll Look at Three Big Questions

The book is planned in three major parts, not because there is any magic in "threes" but because the material falls together around three major questions:

Are you just going through the motions, Dad?

Do you really like being a dad?

Do you know how to be a better dad?

In Part I, I will attempt to do away with three powerful myths that influence a great deal of our thinking about fatherhood: the instant father, the Super Dad, and the well-known cliché, "Love is all they need." The overall goal in these chapters is to help dads tear down some of the false storefronts where popular concepts of fatherhood are often displayed. In trying to fit these popular concepts, it is quite possible to "just go through the motions," and a lot of dads are. It is also possible to understand the real calling and importance of fatherhood and to make our moves really count.

In Part II, I'll take three more chapters to deal with what I believe is a very tough question: "Do I really *like* being a dad?" Stated another way, the question asks, "Do I really like my kids?" Do I take time to see them for who they really are? Do I accept them as they are or do I play the game called "I'll accept you *if* and *when* . . ."?

In this second section we'll also look at the "risk" in fathering and why so many fathers are falling for the "play it safe" fallacy. Here I will explore the countless possibilities in making fatherhood more of an adventure and less of a chore.

In Part III we'll get practical (but I hope you don't skip the first five chapters and miss wrestling with some powerful principles that are designed to raise your consciousness as well as your sights regarding fatherhood). First we look at setting goals and making plans. Then we dig into a gold mine of tips for working the goals and plans that fit you and your style of fathering. Finally, we close our look at what kids need most in a dad by examining three vital things our kids want and need from us: time, consistency, and enthusiasm. And I am quite serious when I say the greatest of these is enthusiasm.

I'm enthusiastic about being a dad. I don't think you will

have to read too far to see that. It's my desire that you catch that same kind of enthusiasm for fathering—for the first time, perhaps, or in a new and greater way than ever before. There is an old poem of unknown origin in my files that is titled simply, "Sharing." One of the stanzas nicely captures my goal for the time you and I will spend together on these pages:

> There isn't much that I can do,
> But I can share my hopes with you,
> And I can share my fears with you,
> And sometimes shed some tears with you
> . . . as on our way we go.

Definition of a Dad

If he's wealthy and prominent, and you stand in awe of him, call him "father." If he sits in his shirt sleeves and suspenders at a ball game and picnic, call him "Pop." If he wheels the baby carriage and carries bundles meekly, call him "Papa" (with the accent on the first syllable). If he belongs to a literary circle and writes cultured papers, call him "Papa" (with the accent on the last syllable).

If, however, he makes a pal of you when you're good, and is too wise to let you pull the wool over his loving eyes when you're not; if, moreover, you're quite sure no other fellow you know has quite so fine a father, you may call him "Dad."

William B. Franklin

From *A Father's Love* by Peter S. Seymour

Part I
Are You Just Going Through the Motions, Dad?

Doing Away With Three Major Myths of Fatherhood

Before determining what kids need most in a dad, it might be worthwhile to look at some things they need *least*. In these first three chapters, we'll take a look at three fallacies of fathering—three myths that we often unconsciously nurture, which can dim our desire, weaken our wills, and undermine our resolve to become the kind of fathers God calls us to be.

The first one is the myth of "instant everything," which has also invaded the family domain. We think we can be fathers in our spare time, or in "just no time at all."

The second one is the well-hyped myth of Super Dad, but when was the last time you saw SERVANT FATHER on a license plate holder?

The third one is more subtle, but perhaps the most dangerous myth of them all. We like to say there are no perfect parents. We may make mistakes, but "love is all they need." Is it?

One
Just Add Water and Mix
The Myth of Instant Fathering

We assume that if something can be done at all, it can be done quickly and efficiently. Our attention spans have been conditioned by thirty-second commercials. Our sense of reality has been flattened by thirty-page abridgments.

Eugene Peterson[1]

Now it has been said that paternity is a career imposed on you one fine morning without any inquiry as to your fitness for it. That is why there are so many fathers who have children, but so few children who have fathers.

Adlai Stevenson[2]

I like to talk to my father about my problems, but when I need him, he's not there. It's like he's a shadow.

Brian, Age Fifteen

There is a terrible untruth going around these days and many of us are believing it. We are caught up in an instant society where we can cook meals in a microwave in only a few minutes, drive a mile in a little over sixty seconds, and turn on a TV set to see news from all over the world as it happens via satellite.

It is an era of instant coffee, instant banking, instant dinners, and instant satisfaction. We all fall prey to the illusion that we can apply the *instant* principle to other parts of our daily lives.

Actually, the *instant* syndrome has been with us for quite a while. I remember, as a young boy, the thrill of being able to throw pancake mix into a bowl and just add water with the confident knowledge that the flapjacks would not end up tasting like cardboard. Likewise, I can remember on some early backpacking trips that preparing food was simply a matter of adding a little H_2O and stirring with a spoon.

At this point in my life, however, I'm not sure that "instant" is the healthiest way to eat. I'm also beginning to wonder if it's a very healthy model for my sons to see and imitate. I fear that they may be picking up an unreal perspective of how the world really works. They may wind up like the city youngster who was visiting his country cousin. The lad from the city spotted some empty milk bottles in the grass. "Come quick, Johnny," he yelled to his cousin. "I've found a cow's nest!"[3]

"In Just No Time at All"

With all of this instant technology as part of our everyday lives and as natural as breathing, we fall into the trap of a very attractive illusion. We come to believe—often unconsciously—that just about anything can happen immediately. We buy into the erroneous idea that even the important processes in our lives are really not that difficult.

What Kids Need Most in a Dad

Learning something or becoming something can be done, we say, "in just no time at all." We become masters at underestimating the demands that life can make upon us.

This kind of thinking has also invaded the family circle. We would like to think that we can become capable and effective fathers while avoiding the work, pain, and process necessary. "Instant father" is an attractive myth. After all, who has less time than a busy father who must spend good parts of his day on the commuter freeways, not to mention eight or more hours in the office, shop, or field.

The trouble is, our penchant for instant parenting isn't working. The deterioration of the family is a well-known problem in our society. Families are breaking down everywhere as parents find that there are no instant answers to the long-term problems. And many experienced family counselors and specialists—Dr. James Dobson among them—insist that the breakdown of the family is due, in large part, to a lack of creative leadership from the father.

It would be easy to roast fathers for their lack of involvement with their children (not to mention neglect of their wives). But I'm not really interested in doing that. The only point that I want to establish here is that there is no magic formula for being a good parent, and there are no shortcuts to that vital commodity called experience.

Who Cares?

Interestingly enough, the ministry in which I have participated for the past thirteen years is dedicated to giving young (and older) people experience in a new and challenging setting. In the late sixties I was teaching in a high school in San Carlos, California, and becoming increasingly concerned about the lack of enthusiasm for life that seemed to hang over many of the students like a mushroom cloud of apathetic unconcern. My frustration grew until one day I walked into class and printed on the board in large—literally two-foot—letters the word A P A T H Y. A particularly laid back senior in the front row squinted up at this strange message, mouthed the word a few times, and then tried to say it aloud.

"A," he muttered (with a long A), "pathy," he finally got it all out.

As I marveled at his unique pronunciation, he turned to his buddy and queried, "Wassat?"

His neighbor glanced at the board without even raising his head, suppressed a yawn, and actually gave this answer: "Who cares?"

I still consider that moment one of the more unforgettable in my teaching career. *I care,* I thought—and something had to be done.

In 1970 my wife, Pam, and I decided to do something about it. For several summers I had worked with Outward Bound, the well-known wilderness survival school that has offered training throughout the world for the past forty years. Outward Bound is a nonreligious, nonsectarian organization, but that summer I asked my director if I could try offering a Christian version of the wilderness program and see if I could get any takers.

"If you can fill it, you can do it," he told me. We did fill it and had a tremendous three weeks, backpacking, rock climbing, learning to survive in unknown situations, and most important, considering together why God had put us on this earth and His will for our lives.

The next summer I left my high school teaching job and went full time to found Summit Expedition, a ministry "dedicated to providing a new and different educational environment to help young people to reach their full capabilities in Christ."

Since that time over six thousand people from age six to seventy-two have participated in our program, which includes everything from climbing mountains, rappelling down cliffs, fording rushing mountain rivers on bridges made of two slender ropes, and surviving overnight alone with one match and lots of faith.[4]

One Thing God Didn't Create

Believe me when I say that a young man or woman who is about to back off a 150-foot cliff in full rappelling gear is anything but apathetic! Thousands of our students have told us verbally or in testimonial letters that their Summit course was one of the most significant experiences of their lives.

One of the finest bits of encouragement I ever received came, however, from a different source. While preparing for a Summit course, I stopped in a rustic cafe in California's Death Valley. As I sat drinking coffee, Gino, the cook, then in his mid eighties, entertained me with story after story of his adventures as an RAF pilot in the Battle for Britain during World War II, as well as many tales of travel around the world.

As he finished each yarn, Gino would say, "These are true American stories, sonny."

Actually, most of the stories hadn't happened in America, but I didn't quibble. I would gaze into Gino's eighty-year-old eyes, which had the sparkle and enthusiasm of a six-year-old, and laugh with delighted fascination.

As I prepared to leave, I said, "Wish I could stay and hear more, Gino, but I have to go. We've got over fifty students with us and we're about to start this course on desert survival. I appreciate talking with you."

As Gino rang up my bill, he said, "One last thing, sonny. Did you know God created everything except one thing? You know what that one thing is?"

I paused and tried to be tactful. "Gino, I'm no theologian,

but there's a rumor out that God created everything."

With calm assurance Gino replied, "Nope." And then those bright eyes twinkled as he said, "God never got around to creating a *substitute for experience.* Go give 'em experience, sonny. Give those kids as much as they can handle. That's what life is all about."

I've often thought about that conversation with Gino in the little cafe in Death Valley. He was right about experience. Oh, I know we can debate with him as to what life is all about, but there is little doubt that experience is crucial. My encounter with Gino is a continual reminder of life's way of providing paradox. I spend a great deal of my time trying to give young people—particularly those sixteen to twenty-five—the kind of experience that will equip them for life's challenges. But as a father, with two boys of my own, I keep seeing my own need for more experience in an art that few ever master.

And How Does One Get Experience?

It takes time to be a good father. It takes effort—trying, failing, and trying again. Any parent can appreciate the old story about the young vice-president who came in to see the crusty old top man, who was retiring. The young man—who was being groomed to take over—asked the wily veteran his secret of success.

The president replied, "Young man, two words: *good decisions!*"

"Thank you very much, sir. But how does one make good decisions?" the young vice-president wanted to know.

"One word, young man: *experience!*"

"Yes sir, but how does one get experience?"

"Two words, young man: *bad decisions!*"[5]

That well-known old story catches the dilemma we parents face. The trouble with being a father (or a mother) is that we have no experience and there is no time to get any. All of a sudden our children are there and we are parents. The race is on and every lap brings a new challenge with a different crisis. And it's a long race. It goes on and on, day after day, year after year. We get tired, discouraged, short of temper. There are few parents who would not confess to having those days when they'd like to at least send the kids somewhere with a one-way ticket. Art Linkletter shares a story with which I can identify at times:

A child wrote a letter to the president of the United States and said, "Dere Mister President. I would like you to send children to Mars in the next space ship going in that direction. I would appreciate it very much if I could go."

The letter was signed, "One of your future voters, Mitchell."

The parents had attached the following note to Mitchell's letter: "Dear Mister President. As the parents of Mitchell Miller, we would like to give you our permission to send Mitchell anywhere into space."[6]

Murphy Must Have Been a Dad

Every parent understands Murphy's First Law: "If anything can go wrong, invariably it will." I like a story I found that describes a scene that could have happened at your house or mine. The father is struggling with the kids to get them to stop clowning around before dinner. Finally, Dad shouts, "All right, let's say grace!"

The kids are right there, completely cooperating as usual. In unison, they shout back, "GRR-ACE!"

Several attempts later, Dad finally settles everyone down. Gathering what is left of his wits, he reverently bows his head and solemnly intones, "Let us play."[7]

The story nicely illustrates the fact that being a parent can be distracting, confusing, and in some cases downright maddening. Parenting is like trying to solve a puzzle when you're not sure you have all the pieces. Parents have to keep remembering that any puzzle worth working takes time and massive doses of patience.

Eugene Peterson has written a fine book on the problem of trying to be a Christian disciple in an instant society. He gets his theme for the book from a quote by philosopher Friedrich Nietzsche, who said, "The essential thing 'in heaven and earth' is . . . that there should be long obedience in the same direction; thereby results, and has always resulted in the long run, something which has made life worth living."[8]

Eugene Peterson has aptly titled his book *A Long Obedience in the Same Direction.* As a Christian father, I see my task as a parent to be exactly that: to be steady and continuing as I seek to obey my heavenly Father in the nurture and training of my children.

Fathering: A Sacred and Difficult Privilege

The Apostle Paul has nicely described the task of long obedience: "Parents, do not treat your children in such a way as to make them angry. Instead, raise them with Christian discipline and instruction" (Ephesians 6:4 TEV). I look into that verse of Scripture and see a tremendous challenge. A father is a man who struggles with what often seems an impossible task. He does not want to exasperate, frustrate, or discourage his kids. At the same time, he wants to train and instruct them. Sometimes, at least for me, it doesn't all go according to the latest handbook on "successful Christian parenting."

It has been said that even God, who is the perfect Father, has children who go astray. A father is a man who agonizes over what he could have done differently and weeps when his children go astray, but who still trusts and hopes that maybe, like the prodigal son, they will return home.

What Kids Need Most in a Dad

Then, too, a father is a man who is *always learning how to love.* He knows that his love must grow and must change because his children change. A father relishes those small moments. He knows what it is like to help with the building of a model airplane, only to have it broken. And he also knows what it is like to help his teenage daughter mend her broken heart when her first romance doesn't work out.

A father knows that everything is important. He knows that nothing is permanent. Each moment counts but no moment counts too much. A father knows how precious time is—not "quality time" but just time—in its fullness and essence. A father is one who realizes the importance of being there to watch his son do his first dive off the high board. A father knows the thrill of watching his daughter ride her bicycle for the first time.

A father also knows the mixed emotions of seeing his teenagers learn how to drive. As he hands them the car keys, he launches them on a new rite of passage. Those keys open the door to a different future for his children, one over which Dad has far less control. The independence he has been trying to develop for so many years has just arrived on a tiny piece of paper stamped "Driver's License." For fathers of newly licensed teenagers, the familiar line from the TV commercial has new meaning: "Now the excitement really begins!"

A father knows the tenderness of having his daughter sit on his lap with her arms around his neck. Then it seems only a few moments later when her arms are around someone else at an altar and she is pledging herself to a new life in which he must play a different—and separate—part.

Fathering Takes Honesty

Above all else, a father is a man who is honest enough to realize that he has to be more than "just a good man."

The Psalmist David, for example, was a very good man—

in fact, "a man after God's heart" (*see* Acts 13:22)—but he struggled deeply in his role as a father. Likewise, Eli the priest was a godly man, but the Scriptures remind us that "the sons of Eli were worthless . . ." (1 Samuel 2:12 NAS). We dare not underestimate the complexity of the task before us. A father is a man who believes that there is a God who gave him his children as a gift and who loves them even more than he does. A Christian father does his best, all the while trusting the Father of all fathers to work His perfect plan in all their lives.

A father is a man who feels and shares and cries, who laughs and wrestles and hopes. He's a man who listens even when he doesn't understand. He's a man who loves even when he feels too weary. He stops doing what he thinks is important to do something else that may be even more important. A father is a man who is honest enough to realize that his responsibilities must determine his priorities.

Back in the foreword, I quoted *The Living Bible* paraphrase of Proverbs 20:7: "It is a wonderful heritage to have an honest father." I read that verse often to remind myself that as a father, I am always giving my children a heritage. I want it to be good and wonderful—and honest. The trouble is that I oftentimes find it difficult to be honest with myself. In a society that allows (and even encourages) game playing, images, stereotypes, performance, and all of the other illusions, I am tempted more frequently than not to join in simply because it's easier. I have to keep remembering that the beginning of being a good father—or a good man—is to be honest, no matter how difficult it is.

There is a basic kind of honesty that I tend to avoid, because it costs too much. Yet I am constantly drawn to embracing that kind of honesty. It's the kind of honesty that pierces the sham of "difficult things can be done instantly." It's the kind of honesty that realizes being a father is not

　　　　　What Kids Need Most in a Dad

merely going through the motions. I can't pretend that fathering is something I can do in my spare time. It's the kind of honesty that realizes that I must make commitments of my time and energy and that I can trust in no easy answers and formulas.

In short, I must make up my mind to really be a father and then get on with it. Chuck Swindoll says it so well:

> *Whatever else may be said about the home, it is the* bottom line *of life, the anvil upon which attitudes and convictions are hammered out. It is the place where life's bills come due, the single most influential force in our earthly existence. No price tag can adequately reflect its value. No gauge can measure its ultimate influence . . . for good or ill. It is at home, among family members, that we come to terms with circumstances. IT IS HERE LIFE MAKES UP ITS MIND.*[9]

We can seriously underestimate the significance of the home. As Swindoll says, the home is the bottom line. Just this morning I was stunned again at the overwhelming importance of the home and the overwhelming importance of my role as a parent. In response I wrote the following "fact sheet" primarily to myself—facts that must be faced honestly, whether I like them or not. They may be appropriate for you as well.

Fact Sheet for Every Dad

Fact 1: I'm a dad. Even on the mornings when I don't feel like it, even when I know I blew it, even when I think I'd rather be doing something else—the central fact of my existence is that I am a husband and a father. There are responsibilities, joys, and sorrows that come with the territory.

What Kids Need Most in a Dad   29

Fact 2: The home is the single most important influence on my family. I can delegate a lot of my responsibilities at work, but I cannot delegate my hopes for my family. The primary values, attitudes, skills, and competencies that my children will grow up with will be learned (or not learned) in my home.

Fact 3: Because of its inherent difficulty and importance, fathering is the most dignified role I will ever play. Over the years, the dignity of fathering has been eroded. Television has portrayed fathers as buffoons, absentee workaholics, or permissive nice guys who don't have a significant value or ethic in their heads.[10] It is no wonder that many men have ceased to devote the kind of time and energy the task of real fathering demands.

Fact 4: Being a parent is one of the greatest sources of joy we can ever know. I really believe that—Murphy's Law not-withstanding. There are the impossible moments, but there are also those moments when fathering is just plain fun.

Fact 5: We all can improve. There are some basic and vital ingredients to good parenting which are essential. We can learn what these are and use them. Parenting is not some esoteric art form that can be understood by only a few. With effort, we can all become much better.

Fact 6: Everyone is unique. Our children are unique and so are we. As we continue to learn from each other, we must accept our uniqueness and discover creative ways to understand and respect one another.

Fact 7: It is difficult to be a good parent. There are no magic potions or formulas. One of the great myths in our society is that we can be parents without real investment of time and energy. The great truth is that there is no substitute for investment of time and effort. If we accept this truth, we are free to transcend the problem. Once we have genuinely realized that being a quality father or mother is difficult, then the problem no longer matters. We can get on with what we have to do. And that is what the rest of this book is all about.

Chapter One Notes

1. Eugene Peterson, *A Long Obedience in the Same Direction* (Downers Grove, Illinois: Inter-Varsity Press, 1980), pp. 11, 12.

2. Peter S. Seymour, *A Father's Love* (Kansas City: Hallmark Books, 1972), p. 5.

3. Art Linkletter, *Kids Say the Darndest Things* (New York: Dale/Caroline Dale Books, published by arrangement with Green Hill Publishers Inc., 1978), p. 4.

4. In recent years we can't even give our students a match, due to fire regulations. But they still go out approximately half a mile from camp to spend the night alone, and they consider it one of the highlights of their wilderness training course.

5. Told in *Tools for Time Management* by Edward R. Dayton (Grand Rapids: Zondervan Publishing House, 1974), pp. 64, 65.

6. Linkletter, *Kids,* p. 13.

7. Adapted from Joseph L. Felix, *Lord, Have Murphy!* (Nashville: Thomas Nelson, Publishers, 1978), p. 13.

8. Friedrich Nietzsche, *Beyond Good and Evil,* trans. Helen Zimmeran (London, 1907), section 188, pp. 106–109.

9. Charles R. Swindoll, *Home: Where Life Makes Up Its Mind* (Portland: Multnomah Press, 1979), p. 5.

10. There are some exceptions, of course. "Little House on the Prairie" is one, and I also liked the father in "The Waltons," even if his wife had a hard time getting him to church.

Two
That's Why God Made Families, Josh!
The Myth of the Super Dad

Learning to live with your family begins with a realistic view of its possibilities and its problems. . . . It helps a great deal if we are not romantically overidealistic on the one hand and not jadedly cynical on the other; family life can and does work but only in the unself-conscious hands of those who understand that it is a continually changing and less than perfect experience.

Eugene Kennedy[1]

I'm so weary of all the images. At church I'm supposed to be some sort of a bionic Christian. At work, I'm supposed to be some kind of a robot. And now at home, I'm expected to be some sort of a Christian Super Dad. It's no wonder that I feel like a failure most of the time. What confuses me is that I thought Christianity was supposed to set us free, instead of tying us up in new knots all the time with impossible expectations. . . .

A Sincere but Frustrated Christian Father

What kind of a man is my dad? Normal, I suppose—and because of that, real special. I can make him laugh, and I've seen him cry. We don't have a lot of money but we sure do a lot of things together. He comes to all my games when he can; he listens to me as if what I had to say was really important. I'll always love him and he'll always love me. I guess that's what it's all about, isn't it? He's no Super Dad; I mean, he makes mistakes, I guess; but in my opinion, if God were to try to assemble a dad who is just right for our family, I think he'd look like my dad.

Brad, Age Sixteen

It was just a little after 5:00 P.M. I was trying to make my weary way home after a very long day. Interstate 10 is the wrong place to be at 5:00 P.M. on most days. They say this freeway extends all the way to Florida, and on this particular occasion I think it was backed up clear from Miami.

L.A.—Lung Abuse, I thought.

For a change of pace I decided to start reading bumper stickers and license plate holders. Some were cute, others were clever, and a few were obscene. One I really liked said: HAVE YOU HUGGED YOUR KID TODAY?

No, I hadn't but I intended to. I couldn't wait to get home. I knew that the boys would attack me as soon as I stepped in the door, and that we would have our usual "world championship wrestling match." I was looking forward to it.

I changed lanes, more for variety in bumper sticker reading than any hope of advancement. I pulled up a little closer to the car in front of me and noticed that its license plate holder said: SUPER DAD.

But the longer I drove behind this SUPER DAD license plate, the more unsure I became of what it really meant. Super Dad. Would I want to be one? What an image to live up to. It sounded like another one of those myths of parenting. Super Dad never gets ruffled. Super Dad always has the answers. Super Dad is in control. He directs and orchestrates—and sometimes, I suppose, he dictates with polish and aplomb.

"Super Dad?" I mused as I turned onto the off ramp. "No thanks. I'm just glad to be a dad. What a privilege, what a responsibility. Maybe I could try to be a *superb* dad—but that's something different."

Home—Where Servant Leadership Is Needed Most

I've seen a lot more SUPER DAD signs since that traffic jam on I-10. Often they're on cars that also carry the sign of the fish, which should be no surprise. If anyone gets pressured to be a Super Dad, it's the Christian father. We are told that we're called to be "head" of the household. We are to manage our kids with efficiency, authority, and never miss a beat—sort of like a corporation president. I'm aware that the Bible calls the man of the house the head and that he should fill that role in the same way Christ is the Head of the church (Ephesians 5:23–28). But was Jesus ever called Super Head? I think He would have disappointed today's PR experts and sign makers. Yes, He was head of the body (His church). And yes, men and women did call Him "Master." But He did His leading in the form of a servant. He told His disciples quite firmly, "Anyone wanting to be a leader among you must be your servant. And if you want to be right at the top, you must serve like a slave. Your attitude must be like my own, for I, the Messiah, did not come to be served, but to serve, and to give my life as a ransom for many" (Matthew 20:26–28 TLB).

For a long time now, I've been comparing the myth of the Super Dad with the concept of servant leadership. One of the reasons this book was written is my belief that the principles of servant leadership should be transferred into the home. Where else is leadership more important? Where else is servanthood more needed?

And so, I've been trying to learn to be a servant father. Frankly, sometimes it's tougher than trying to be a Super Dad. It often reminds me of the inspiration for Charles Sheldon's Christian classic *In His Steps.* You have probably read the story. One hundred people in a typical church in a little town, that could be yours or mine, decided that for one year they would live by one simple rule. They would preface every attitude and every action with the question: "What would Jesus do in this situation?"[2]

I began asking that simple question of myself. What would Jesus do in my home, in the situations I face? I'm sure He wants me to be a servant leader, not a Super Dad. And more than anything else, I think He wants me to let Him be who He is in my life and in my household.

God speaks to all of us in unique and special ways. He sometimes speaks to me most profoundly through tiny incidents and special moments with my children. One such incident last summer has served to remind me of the intrinsic and distilled wonder and holiness of the family. Times like this help me remember that it is in the context of everyday life that God reveals Himself most exquisitely.

Zac, the Eight-Year-Old Theologian

During the summers, our family lives in a little trailer at our base camp in the Sierra Nevada mountain range where we conduct our ministry called Summit Expedition. It was midmorning. I was sitting at the table sipping my second cup of coffee when I overheard Joshua, who was then five, talking with his eight-year-old brother, Zachary. Seeing a picture of Jesus that we had on the trailer wall, he asked a simple and profound question: "Zac, is that what Jesus looks like?"

After a slight hesitation, Zac responded abruptly: "No. He's dead, silly."

What Kids Need Most in a Dad

But then he got a rather sheepish look on his face, especially as he looked over at us.

"Well, no, Josh. He's not exactly dead."

By now, Joshua was justifiably confused, so he asked for a clarification. "Well, is He or isn't He?"

At this, Zac paused reflectively and then continued as only an eight-year-old could: "Well, you see, Josh, He died about two thousand years ago . . . I think it was in 1941. They crucified Him, you see—so that we could be free. He died for our sins. Do you understand?"

Pam and I were amazed at his midget theology, although we're still not sure where he got the date of 1941. Then after another pause, Zac continued: "But then, you see, He rose again, Josh. So, He's not really dead. That's what Easter means. He's alive and He's here."

Joshua, by now, wasn't really sure if he understood but he nodded anyway and then returned to his original question. "Well, then, Zac, how do we know what He looks like?"

At this point, Zac wasn't sure what to do. There was a long pause as he looked at Pam and me. I could see the wheels were turning; he was trying to think of a way to get off the hook. Finally, he said quickly, "Let's pray!"

I bowed my head along with Pam and had mixed feelings of amusement and amazement. Zac had found the perfect escape hatch: a prayer. But it turned out I was wrong. His prayer was genuine. We all found ourselves talking to our heavenly Father. I was deeply touched. But the most memorable line was yet to come. After Zac said, "Amen," he lifted his head quietly. He looked around at all of us and then looked squarely at Joshua.

"Josh, we can know what Jesus looks like."

"How, Zac?" his little brother asked with great excitement.

"That's why God made families, Josh," answered Zac simply.

What Kids Need Most in a Dad

Never have I heard a more profound reason for the value of the family. In his innocence, Zachary had touched upon one of the most important reasons God made families: so that we can continue to discover at the deepest possible level "what He looks like" and who He really is.

Isn't it possible, I thought later, that God reveals Himself most quietly and most profoundly in our own homes? Isn't it possible that the Christian home is the very place where we discover God in the framework of truth and love? Could it be that the family is the sacred place, along with the church, where our children get an X ray of sorts into what God is really like? Could it be that amid all the daily complications, amid all the frustrations and hopes, amid all the tedium and interruptions, the pricelessness of God is revealed daily if we but have eyes to see Him?

In Mark 8:23–25, we can read the story of how Jesus healed a blind man. After He touched him, Jesus asked, " 'Do you see anything?' He looked up and said, 'I see people; they look like trees walking around.' Once more Jesus put his hands on the man's eyes. Then his eyes were opened, his sight was restored, and he saw everything clearly" (NIV).

So, we see that when Jesus touched the man's eyes *a second time,* he saw people as Christ saw them. Could it be that we need a "second touch" whereby God touches our hearts and minds so that we can see our families in a different light? If we let Him, Jesus will turn us into servant leaders—servant fathers, if you please—who "rule" with a different kind of love and authority. A servant father realizes that being a dad is a journey and not a race. In a society that is almost suffocated by its fast pace and prepackaged images, sometimes it becomes increasingly difficult to hear God's voice and respond to His rhythm in our lives —but it is not impossible. More than anything else, a servant father wants to be like Jesus.

And a servant father wants to lead like Jesus. Simply

What Kids Need Most in a Dad

defined, a leader is a man who has followers. We are called to be strong leaders in our homes, where our children are watching us even more carefully than we realize. While the Scripture reference may not be running through their minds, our families are watching us to see if we have come, not to be served, but to serve and give our lives for their benefit (Mark 10:45).

As Richard Foster says in *The Celebration of Discipline,* "The path is fraught with severe difficulties, but also with incredible joys. As we travel on this path, the blessings of God will come upon us and reconstruct us into the image of His Son Jesus Christ."[3]

Just What Does a Servant Father Do?

At this point, you might be thinking (and rightly so), *All this servant leadership sounds very good and biblical, but just what does a servant father actually* do? That's a fair question and I'm still struggling with it myself. Here are some preliminary conclusions that I've come to:

1. *A servant father is more concerned with how he "sees" than with how he "looks."* In other words, my primary role is not to be the boss and just look good but to be a servant leader who enables and enhances my family to be their best. A servant leader sees things through the eyes of his followers. He is an enabler who helps them make their dreams come true rather than just live out his own dreams and ambitions through his children.

2. *A servant father does not say, "Get going," but instead he says, "Let's go."* He leads the way by walking, not behind his children with the whip, nor out in front with the banner, but beside them with support.

3. *A servant father listens as much as he speaks.* He realizes that God gave him two ears and only one mouth, and

that's indicative of something. He doesn't give orders; he creates plans. He doesn't hold his children down; he lifts them up. I believe that one of the greatest things I can do for my children is to lift their spirits by simply listening to their feelings and letting them know I understand.

4. *A servant father is not a "Mr. Fix It."* Instead of solving all his kids' problems for them, he works with them to help them learn how to solve their own problems. He realizes that if his children are to learn to be good decision makers, they need to start early by making their own choices. So, he's willing to take the time necessary to help them learn those skills and attitudes.

5. *A servant father recognizes that his children are a gift from God.* "Behold, children are a gift of the Lord" (*see* Psalms 127:3). He recognizes them as a treasure and not an obligation, a privilege and not just a duty. How often we hear dads complaining about what a hassle having kids is. These fathers seem to see only the difficulties and problems in parenting. But the servant father works with bold gladness as he realizes that in God's hidden logic, he is called to lead by serving and serve while leading.

6. *The servant father realizes that weakness is the prerequisite of power.* Moses knew something about realizing power through admitting weakness. When God gave him the overwhelming assignment to lead His people out of Egypt, he resisted because he thought he wasn't adequate for the task. "O Lord, I never have been eloquent, neither in the past nor since you have spoken to your servant. I am slow of speech and tongue" (Exodus 4:10 NIV). But even as Moses declared his weakness, it became the very vehicle of God's supply of strength and sufficiency.

The same thing happened in Paul's life. The apostle pleaded with God to take his weakness from him but God only said, "My grace is sufficient for you, for my power is made perfect in weakness" (2 Corinthians 12:9 NIV).

Throughout Scripture, God is seen using the weak and the foolish to accomplish His purposes. Our very power as servant fathers comes not from our own abilities but from God. It is only when we realize our own weakness that we can truly draw on our resources in the Holy Spirit. And it is then that we discover what it means to be a servant father.

7. *A servant father has a sense of humor.* He can laugh at himself because he has a humble spirit. He laughs because he has a sane estimate of who he is. He knows he doesn't have to be Super Dad. He can be himself instead of brittle and rigid. He takes fathering very seriously but he doesn't take himself too seriously.

I know what that kind of battle can be like. In my previous book I wrote:

> *This struggle became so real for me that I have found I need constant reminders to help me be free in Jesus Christ and not to take myself too seriously. So, I carry small toys—a tiny Snoopy, or King Kong, or little squatty hippo, or any such object that I can get into my pocket. Those who know me well know that they're in the pockets of most of my coats and virtually all of my trousers. They sit on my desk and they are by my books. They serve as a constant reminder not only of my children and how much I love them, but that I too am a child of God, and that He loves me, and I don't have to waste time taking myself too seriously.[4]*

8. *A servant father can also be led.* He is not interested in having his own way but in finding the best way. He's a man with an open mind who keeps his eyes on his high goals

and strives to meet them with every ounce of energy that God has given him. He is not afraid of failure or change.

9. *A servant father is a man who prays.* Dr. James Dobson tells the story of his grandfather who, over a stretch of eleven years, prayed for one hour each day for the salvation of his children and grandchildren. Since then, not only have all his children and grandchildren become Christians but many are also in full-time Christian ministry.

I must confess, I'm not up to one hour a day, but I do wear a little green sticker on my watch to remind me to pray for my family. Dozens of times each day I'm reminded to pray not only for their wholeness in Christ but also for their health, their safety, their dreams, their education, and their joy in living. Above all, that little sticker reminds me to be thankful for the gift of my family.

These nine points may sound rather formidable. Some of them even have a dramatic touch. But servant leadership isn't always dressed up in dramatic acts, as the following story shows.

The Rocked-Out Servant Father

A few weeks ago I was with Ben Parks, a dear friend who is a living example of what it means to be a servant leader. On the job he's a teacher and a coach. At home, he lives out the role of servant father. On that particular day he had started with the first rays of the sun. I had been with him much of the day and had seen him pour his life into many young people. That evening, we went to his home for dinner and he told me that after dinner we would be going to see his daughters, Jeri Ann and Rhonda, sing at their school's senior concert. I nodded agreement, little realizing what we were getting into.

The senior "concert" was a rock music affair, where the

students didn't sing, but pantomimed the loudest records they could find. Ancient malfunctioning speakers that roared, grated, and tweaked didn't help matters either.

The gym was obnoxiously loud and sweaty. The teenagers mingled and gyrated to a music that I had long since forgotten how to enjoy. But Ben and I laughed. I told him, "You owe me one—when my kids get old enough for this kind of thing, I'm going to drag you to one of these, too." And we laughed again.

Ben had complained about a headache on the way down to the concert. The noise that was supposed to be music had to be increasing his pain to Excedrin levels, but he just sat on the edge of his seat, waiting for his daughters to perform. They finally came on and as soon as he saw them, he stood up in the middle of the gym and started yelling at the top of his lungs, "Way to go, Jeri Ann! Way to go, Rhonda!" I could barely hear him shouting above the din, but Jeri Ann and Rhonda saw him and I could tell they were pleased.

Later, on the way home in the car, I started thinking about Ben at the concert. How true it is that a servant father is one who stays involved in the lives of his children, even when his voice can't be heard. A servant father is one who attends his children's functions, even when he has to sit on hard bleachers.

That rock concert had been anything but Handel's *Messiah,* but I nonetheless felt that I had just attended church and seen one of the more powerful sermons ever preached. Ben could easily have stayed home. He had plenty of excuses and even some good reasons. But instead, he chose to serve his kids. He had indeed followed the example of his Lord, who on that fateful night before He was crucified, ". . . got up from the supper table, took off his robe, wrapped a towel around his loins, poured water into a basin, and began to wash the disciples' feet and to wipe

What Kids Need Most in a Dad   43

them with the towel he had around him" (John 13:4, 5 TLB).

In short, the servant father is willing to make constant, daily sacrifices for those he loves. I discovered recently that the word *sacrifice* doesn't mean "to give up." The original language actually means, "to make holy." Servant fathers make their homes a holy place through small acts of service and leadership that may not even be noticed. Servant fathers continue to be involved in the lives of their families even when they don't have the time, energy, or inclination. Servant fathers continue to love their children even when they fail.

My own father would never have qualified as a Super Dad. But I still vividly remember the night he played the role of servant father with unforgettable style.

"Are You Wondering Where Your Son Is?"

Throughout their lives my mother and dad quietly gave even when they didn't see the results. They both had to make numerous sacrifices as my brother and I were growing up. Mom and Dad both worked two jobs in order to help make ends meet.

My brother, Steve, was a fine student and president of his senior class. I tried to follow in his footsteps, although I had a wilder bent at times. I worked hard to be a good student and a good athlete. I even made student body president, which was partly due to some successes on the football field. In my senior year I was voted "All City" and "All State."

On the night of one of my greatest triumphs, however, I failed my father miserably, and it was then that he demonstrated his ability as a servant leader. We had just won our final football game, which meant that we would be going to the State Championship. Some of us had been informed that we would repeat as all league selections for a second year. We decided that all of this success was worthy of celebration. So, many of us football players got together and truly celebrated—a bit too hard. Somewhere we had gotten some beer, and according to our high school logic, we thought that the more we drank the more we were celebrating. We drank too much.

A policeman happened to drive by and spot us in a parking lot behind some stores. Doing his job, he came over to investigate and discovered that more than a few of us were quite thoroughly inebriated.

The policeman put in a call for some help. Then, in my opinion, he started pushing around some of my friends. Because I was student body president, I felt it was my job to defend them and I ended up trying to wrestle with the cop. That was not a good idea.

The next thing the cop called for was a paddy wagon. Twenty minutes later we were all on our way to jail. That night was one of the longest I've ever spent. At about five the next morning—just about the time the newspaper was being delivered to our home with my picture in it for being an All City and All State athlete—my parents received a phone call from the chief of police.

"Mr. and Mrs. Hansel, are you wondering where your son is? I'm phoning from the city jail and I would like you to come down here and pick up your son."

I can imagine how long that drive downtown was for my folks. When they arrived, they saw a group of dejected young men. Other parents also arrived and had to face the same kind of disappointment. Their sons, who just a few hours before had been a source of such great pride, had all failed so miserably.

My mom and dad walked in and I'll never forget the moment when their eyes met mine. They must have been wondering if all their sacrifices had been worth it. But they never spoke a word.

We got in the car. The sun was coming up and tears were

rolling down my cheeks. Finally, I could take the silence no longer and blurted, "Aren't you going to say something, Dad?"

After a pause that probably seemed longer than it really was, my dad finally spoke. "Sure . . . let's go have some breakfast, *son."*

Those were the only words he uttered. At a time when I had failed him most tragically, he reminded me that I was his son. At a time when I felt the deepest remorse and a total failure, he said, in effect, "Let's get on with it."

In the years that followed, he never once brought up that incident. He simply continued to love me for who I was and who I could be.

A Super Dad? Not really. He had all kinds of rough edges and some very real flaws.

A servant father? Indeed.

Chapter Two Notes

1. Eugene Kennedy, *Living with Everyday Problems* (Chicago: Thomas More Press, 1974), pp. 63, 64.

2. Charles L. Sheldon, *In His Steps* (Grand Rapids: Zondervan Publishing House, 1967).

3. Richard Foster, *The Celebration of Discipline* (San Francisco: Harper & Row Publishers, Inc., 1978), p. 7.

4. Tim Hansel, *When I Relax I Feel Guilty* (Elgin, Illinois: David C. Cook Publishing Co., 1979), p. 87.

What Kids Need Most in a Dad

Three
Just Love Ain't Always Enough
The Myth of "Love Is All They Need"

The flood of change about to crash down upon us will spread from universities and research centers to factories and offices, from the marketplace and the mass media into our social relationships, from the community into the home. Penetrating deep into our private lives, it will place absolutely unprecedented strains on the family itself.

Alvin Toffler[1]

With my dad, I learn more than I do anywhere else. I learn the important things in life—how to fix things, have patience, and learn to take time to do things correctly. He teaches me all the things I need for survival in the future. . . .

Greg, Age Seventeen

My prayer for you is that you may have still more love—a love that is full of knowledge and wise insight.

Paul the Apostle[2]

J.B. Phillips's above translation of Philippians 1:9 gave me courage to tackle what could be the most deceiving myth of all regarding fatherhood. This myth is deceiving because it sounds so right. As moms and dads grope through the thick fog of parenting problems, they often flee to their last bastion of security. We may fail to fulfill the image of Super Dad (or Super Mom). We may fall short of servant leadership. But we can always hold tight to the idea of what really matters—the absolute bottom line—love. "Love," we say, almost with a sigh of relief, "is really all they need, and *surely* I try to give them *that!*"

I understand that kind of statement. I've made it myself many times. When I talk about a myth called "love is all they need" I'm not saying we should love our children less. As Paul put it, "My prayer for you is that you may have *still more love.*" Paul was directing that prayer to Christians of all ages in the church at Philippi, but I think it has particular application to Christians today—especially Christian parents. Our children, in particular, need more love—a powerful, tenacious, understanding, discerning kind of love.

Maybe one of the reasons most of us don't love more is that we think we already love enough. But in many homes, we face a crisis caused by what might be called a "love gap." I'm still one of those who believes that a time of crisis brings the greatest opportunity. The Chinese understand this. If you separate the two Chinese characters that spell the word *crisis,* you get the words *dangerous opportunity.* In the most real sense, there never has been a time of greater opportunity to do more loving within the family circle.

How loving is your family circle, Dad? I ask myself the same question, especially when I hear about one university study that calls the American home the most dangerous place to be, outside of riots and war.[3] There is more domes-

What Kids Need Most in a Dad

tic violence today than ever before. In his book *Improving Your Serve,* Chuck Swindoll writes:

> *No less than 30 percent of all American couples experience some form of domestic violence in their lifetimes. This helps explain why 20 percent of all police officers killed in the line of duty are killed while answering calls involving family fights, and why it is estimated that anywhere from six to fifteen million* women *are battered in our nation each year.*[4]

Granted, a lot of fathers could say, "Well, that's not *my* home. Nobody gets battered in my family." Unfortunately, other dangers still assault our homes from all sides. They particularly sneak in on the airwaves through our television and radio sets. They also come in through the front door in the form of magazines and newspapers. I'm talking about the impact of media advertising on all of us. Consumerism is the prevailing philosophy of our society. We are urged to spend and spend and use and use and buy and buy, turning the dollars over and over to keep the economy going. I don't want to argue economics, but I am concerned about what all this is doing to the self-esteem of our children.

The "You're Not Okay" Syndrome

It is estimated that a young person may see, hear, or read as many as fifty thousand media messages each year, which come through television and radio commercials, magazine and newspaper ads, and the like. Some of the best minds in the country are working on these ads and commercials, and many of them are designed to communicate one central message: "You're not okay."

We often fail to understand the power of all this because it is so subtle. But the total impact of all of this media input is much like someone poking us or shoving us hundreds of times a day and saying, "Do you know what? You're really not okay just as you are. If you don't get this certain kind of toothpaste, or wear this special brand of jeans . . . if you don't drive this kind of car, or use this kind of deodorant or mouthwash . . . then you're really not okay."

During major events, such as the Super Bowl or the final episode of "M*A*S*H," it can cost almost a million dollars a minute to buy advertising time on television. No wonder the advertisers bring in the most sophisticated brains in the country to help convince all of us who are watching that we're incomplete or unfulfilled without their product.

But parents can make a difference. We can teach our kids to turn off the tube more often and cut down the number of negative messages they get each day. But even more important, we can teach our kids to analyze those messages and understand why the nice man or the pretty lady keeps saying things like, "I can raise my hands with *confidence!*"

And above all, we can give our kids increasing amounts of assurance and esteem. We can send them messages many times a day that say, "You are *okay.*"

The Future Shock Syndrome

Since I'm for loving my kids with all I've got, you may be wondering why I'm concerned about the myth I call "love is all they need." I'm concerned because I wonder. In these times of incredible upheaval and change is "just love" enough? As powerful as hugs and "I love yous" are, is it really all they need?

Coming back to the Apostle Paul for a moment, let's take a closer look at what he wrote to the Philippian Christians. "My prayer for you," Paul said, "is that you may have still

What Kids Need Most in a Dad

more love—a love that is full of knowledge and wise insight" (Philippians 1:9 PHILLIPS). I'd like to emphasize those words: *full of knowledge and wise insight.* If ever we needed knowledge and wise insight it is now, not so much to cope with the present, which is bad enough, but to survive the future, which will be so difficult and demanding that it can boggle your mind. The basic question that I really want to ask in this chapter is, *Are you adequately preparing your children for a future that will be far different from anything any of us have ever known?*

Some of that future shock is already here. You know the grim statistics on divorce rates: almost one out of two marriages goes on the rocks. What is even more sobering, however, is that the suicide rate among teenagers has more than doubled since 1956. Why is all this happening? Again, the pervasive forces that are working on us are so subtle that we don't really see them or understand them.

I'm very serious when I say that every father should read books like *Future Shock* and *Megatrends.*[5] *Future Shock* was written by Alvin Toffler, professional writer and specialist on "sociology of the future." *Future Shock* was a best-seller in the 1970s and much of what Toffler predicted is already coming to pass. Toffler wrote his book with the explicit goal of helping people ". . . come to terms with the future—to help us cope more effectively with personal and social change by deepening our understanding of how men respond to it."[6]

Just a few of the pressures Toffler describes include the accelerating pace of life, our emphasis on things in a throwaway society, and mankind's new nomadic existence. Every year we learn how to move from one end of the earth to the other faster than ever before. Some people seem to live in a constant state of jet lag. Toffler also talks about the information overload that bombards everybody. Quite frankly, we are already being hit with so much information and overchoice that it is getting harder and harder for many people to make decisions. What will it be like for our children?

The population explosion is also part of the future shock syndrome. Toffler points out that in 1850 only four cities over the entire earth had 1 million or more people. By 1900, 19 cities had populations of 1 million or more. By 1960 there were 141 cities and in the latter part of the twentieth century the numbers are still climbing. According to Toffler, ". . . today world urban population is rocketing upward at a rate of 6.5 percent per year. . . . This single stark statistic means a doubling of the earth's urban population within eleven years."[7]

In a follow-up to *Future Shock,* Toffler wrote *The Third Wave,* a description of how the world began with an agricultural society, which lasted from roughly 8000 B.C. to the first half of the eighteenth century. According to Toffler, somewhere around the 1950s we moved into what he calls the "third wave" of human history—which can be symbolized by the introduction of the computer as well as many other technological advancements. For the last thirty years the computer has already made an enormous impact on our society. In 1980 Toffler wrote:

> *Outside the confines of industry and government, moreover, a parallel process is underway based on that soon-to-be-ubiquitous gadget: the home computer. Five years ago the number of home or personal computers was negligible. Today it is estimated that 300 thousand computers are whirring and buzzing away in living rooms, kitchens and dens from one end of America to the next. And this is before the major manufacturers, like I.B.M. and Texas Instruments, launched their sales drives. Home computers will soon be selling for little more than a television set.[8]*

What Kids Need Most in a Dad

And we have seen Toffler's prophecy come true many-fold. "Apples," "Wangs," and other computer brands have become household standbys in millions of homes. And where are all these shocks and waves of the future taking us? What are they actually doing to people?

In his best-selling book *Megatrends,* John Naisbitt tries to make sense of everything that is going on by categorizing it into ten new directions that are transforming our lives. One of Naisbitt's most provocative chapters is one in which he describes his formula of "high tech versus high touch." Here Naisbitt describes the backlash that is already occurring against computers and other technology. People are reacting vehemently against the impersonal quality of being a number on somebody's terminal many miles away.

Naisbitt believes that all of the "high tech" developments that we've seen over the last fifteen to twenty years have caused, in great part, the tremendous acceleration of the human potential movement. People want to be with people, not machines. And so, they have developed "high touch," the philosophy that has people banding together—at work, at school, in small groups, discussion groups—anything to hold off the feelings of frustration and emptiness that come from seeing your life controlled by electronic circuits and computer printouts. As Naisbitt writes:

> The more technology we introduce into society, the more people will aggregate, will want to be with other people: movies, rock concerts, shopping. Shopping malls, for example, are now the third most frequented space in our lives, following home and work place. [9]

In the paragraphs above I have given only the briefest sketch of what the future shocks and megatrends are doing to us and will be doing to us in the next generations. And that is why—devoted to loving my kids as I am—I wonder if love is all they need. I wonder if John Naisbitt is not echoing Paul's words about the need for knowledge and wise insight when he writes in *Megatrends,* "We must learn to balance the material wonders of technology with the spiritual demands of our human nature."[10]

That's why I believe that as a father I must not only be deeply concerned with loving my children with plenty of affection and affirmation; I must also be training them in at least four key areas. These areas include skills, attitudes, values, and competencies. In these four words lie what I believe is at least part of what Paul means by ". . . knowledge and wise insight."

Attitudes, Skills, and "How To"

When we talk about knowledge, we cannot limit our concept to "more information." As we can quickly see, today's society is already overloading us with more facts, news items, and media experiences than we can possibly process. I like to define *knowledge* as, among other things, "know-how"—the ability to solve problems and learn how to work responsibly. As our children face future shocks, third waves, and megatrends, they must develop new attitudes and skills to cope with life. They must know how to attack problems, break them down into workable size, and solve them creatively.

Again, television looms as one of our most formidable stumbling blocks in this area. As our children watch television, they are told many times a day, subconsciously of course, that it takes only thirty minutes to solve most problems, while the more difficult problems might take a full hour. It is no wonder, then, that many children become severely frustrated when they discover the reality of how long it takes to solve real problems in real life.

The young have never been known for great patience, but today their impatience and frustration can be seen on every hand. One of the things I remember from my college psychology course is that frustration is the source of anger, and the second state of frustration, following anger, is apathy. First we get frustrated and become angry. Then, if we can't solve the problem through our anger, we become apathetic. It takes no sociological guru to observe that there is a good deal of frustration, anger, and apathy in our churches, schools, and homes. Is it really hard for us to understand why the kids go to drugs and booze as a way to cope with life?

We Need an Attitude Overhaul

If our children are to be better problem solvers, we must help them cultivate some stronger attitudes. For example:

- Problems are not "bad" or abnormal—they are a continuing part of daily life.
- Problems can be solved—if we are willing to work at them.

I believe that another pervasive message our children receive from the media is that problems are something people shouldn't have. Many TV heroes are "Mr. Fix Its" who conquer the bad guys or save the situation and then ride into the sunset on their Nighthawks or black Trans Ams. Our kids are growing up believing that problems are temporary blips on the screen—nothing to be worried about as they wait for the easy answers and the easy out.

Adults aren't immune, either. In his wonderful little book *Living With Everyday Problems,* Eugene Kennedy writes, " 'If

I can just get through this problem, then everything will be all right,' may be one of the most common English sentences." But, says Kennedy, "there comes a time, and it may well be the birth of maturity—when we suddenly realize that if we do get through our present problem, there will be another one, slightly larger and a little more intense, waiting to take its place."[11]

When we finally grow up we realize life is one series of problems after another. Some are homely and familiar. Some are difficult and complex. Some are even exotic and bizarre. And the better problem solvers our kids are, the more capable they will be to meet these ongoing problems of the future. Their lives will be a continuing response to the inevitable problems that go along with their journey toward adulthood and maturity. And yet, I know very few dads who are making a truly conscious effort to teach their kids how to solve problems.

We can always blame it on the changing times. In past generations, kids would grow up with their dad on the farm. They learned to solve problems naturally as they fixed the tractor, built the addition to the chicken coop, or extended the irrigation ditch. But today, we live in cities and suburbs where our problems are both more blatant and more subtle.

I am frequently asked to give seminars on creative problem solving. I am often appalled by how little we know about the attitudes, principles, and process involved in learning how to be a better problem solver. As we have seen, the right attitude is basic. I believe that problems are good things. Problems are God-given opportunities to grow. They are the very challenges which drive us to deeper understanding and maturity. Few people realize, for example, that the word *problem* comes from the Greek root *pro balein,* which actually means "to throw or drive forward." Problems drive us forward. Some people are able to make problems into challenges and opportunities, whereas others seem to convert almost all their opportunities into "problems."

Lying right at the core of anyone's problem-solving ability is his or her attitude. Those who say they can and those who say they can't are both right. I was almost thirty years old before I realized that I could be a good problem solver, *if I wanted to be.* It began for me with a challenge, when somebody simply asked me why I couldn't become a better problem solver. So, I made the decision to become the very best problem solver I could be.

Once you gain the right attitude toward problem solving, you need to develop some skills. These skills really aren't that difficult to learn. Most of the excellent books on problem solving usually boil down to some basic steps that everyone can take.[12]

Six Steps for Problem Solvers

1. *The first step in problem solving—believe it or not—is* accepting *the problem.* Many people don't become good problem solvers because they avoid admitting there really is a problem. You take your first step when you face reality and see that there is indeed a problem. And not only that —*you make a decision to commit the necessary time and energy to solve it.*

2. *The second step involves* orienting *yourself to the problem.* All good problem-solving approaches remind us that we must understand the problem from as many angles as possible. We need to break the problem down into logical parts. We need to analyze it as carefully as possible, seeing and observing as much as we can.

3. *The third step—possibly the most important—is to* define *the problem in the best terms that we know how.*

Most good problem solvers say that once you have adequately defined the problem, you are well over halfway to solving it.

Defining problems accurately is a skill that takes a great deal of time to develop. When I see my two boys coming home crying or frustrated, or even apathetic and bored with school, I try to ask them, "Well, what really is the problem?" After we talk about it for a while, it's amazing to see their eyes light up as they realize what the problem really is. As they define their problem—in their own words and terms—they are often capable of solving their problems on their own.

4. *Once the problem is defined clearly, the fourth step is to creatively* brainstorm *as many possible solutions and approaches to the problem as you can.* Dads can have a great time trying to help their children figure out creative approaches to problems they may be facing—the recent disagreement with the best friend down the block, their difficulties with schoolwork, why they are playing on the second team instead of the first team, why they never seem to have enough money, and so on and so on.

I'm trying to realize that I must allow my children to accept their own problems. I can't go around constantly fixing problems for them. Instead, I want to give them the skills and attitudes they need to learn to solve problems on their own. It doesn't do them any good (or me for that matter) to lose my cool over their inability to solve a problem and then step in to solve it for them. Problem solving is one of the most important skills I want them to learn as they grow up.

5. *The fifth step in problem solving is to* select *one of the many ideas that have been suggested.* After you help your children think of every resource and possibility they can use to solve a problem, you need to guide them in making a decision and implementing that decision. This part of the

process can lead to a lot of good, healthy dialogue between you and your children as you talk about what ideas will work and won't work. Dads have an advantage in years and experience that can be helpful in guiding their children to make the best choices and then actually going ahead and trying out the solution. Remember, however, to always try to see it from your child's point of view. What may seem like the best or easiest solution to you may not be easy for your child. Don't jam your solution down his throat. If you do, you are simply back to playing Mr. Fix It again.

6. *The final step is* evaluation. Did the solution to the problem work or not? After your children have given the problem their best shot, get together with them and measure the results. Did the solution fail or succeed? If the solution failed, help your children realize that that is all that failed—the *idea* failed, *they* did not. Help them realize that when solving problems, failure is a natural part of the process. Help them retrace their steps back through the problem solving that they have done and to analyze where it went wrong. Help them define the problem still more accurately and select another idea. I repeat, emphasize that because one solution fails, it doesn't make your children failures. A failure is someone who quits or gives up. The successful person keeps trying many solutions until the right one works.

I'm very serious when I say teaching problem-solving attitudes and skills to our children is one of the most important things we can do to equip them for the future. This is why I say that "just love ain't always enough." We must equip our kids with know-how, the kind of knowledge that demonstrates itself in proper attitudes and skills.

We Also Need Wise Insight

There is one more thought left in Paul's word to the Philippians that is worth at least a brief look by every dad. Paul wants us to have love, a love full of knowledge "... and wise insight ... to be able always to recognise the highest and best ..." (Philippians 1:9 PHILLIPS). My children not only need the right attitudes and skills but they also need the right values and competencies.

I want my kids to have strong, biblical values as they move into the exciting but unstable future. And I want them to be competent, with the kind of maturity and character that does not fail under pressure. The writer to the Hebrews says it so beautifully in the final verses of the tenth chapter. J.B. Phillips includes a subhead here that says, "Recollect your former faith, and stand firm today!" Phillips then goes on to translate:

> You must never forget those past days when you had received the light and endured such a great and painful struggle.... Don't throw away your trust now—it carries with it a rich reward. Patient endurance is what you need if, after doing God's will, you are to receive what he has promised.
> For yet a very little while,
> He that cometh shall come, and shall not tarry.
> But my righteous one shall live by faith;
> And if he shrink back, my soul hath no pleasure in him.
> Surely we are not going to be men who cower back and are lost, but men who maintain their faith for the salvation of their souls!
>
> *Hebrews 10:32, 35–39 PHILLIPS*

If I want my children to have the biblical values that help them not to shrink back under the demands of their future, I must begin now. It is never too late to start doing what is right. The distinctive mark of Christians in the future is that they will be people who have values that will not fade under the inevitable stress and pressure. And as they complement these values with the right attitudes and skills, they will succeed in developing competencies with which they may serve the Lord Jesus Christ and the world with wise discernment. Wisdom and discernment come from a knowledge that is embedded in deep values which are settled in the living God. Wisdom is the quality of being able to make the right use of knowledge. Wisdom is spiritual perception grounded in the common sense of the very Word of God.

My boys, Zac and Josh, have both won Bibles in their daily vacation Bible school classes. Perhaps your children have done the same, or you may have presented them with their own Bibles a long time ago. It's going to take our children a long time to understand fully the contents of those Bibles. For that matter, we parents are still trying to understand the Scriptures ourselves. How then can we possibly teach them all they need to know? Many dads grope here, almost blindly, because they don't consider themselves experts, with the "gift of teaching," or of being verbal regarding the Scriptures.

I think there is tremendous encouragement in a basic fact about kids. They learn best by example. Your attitude toward material possessions, toward other people, toward education, toward curiosity, toward spiritual matters will be "caught" by your children more than it will be taught. Do your kids see you taking time out to read the Bible? Do they see you allowing the Word of God to seep into your life and your behavior? Do your kids see you trusting God even when things go wrong? Growing up is never easy and what your kids see in your life is often more important than what they hear.

Wisdom, discernment, and wise insight come from spending time with God. Then you transmit that wisdom, discernment, and wise insight to your children by spending time with them. And as your children run into the inevitable problems of growing up, they can see you leading them with the kind of patience that endures, the kind of discernment that seeks God's best instead of simply looking for the easy way out and the short-range (often shortsighted) solution.

Paul Anderson has put together a marvelous little book called *Building Christian Character.* In the foreword, Larry Christenson writes:

> *We live in a day when image rates higher than character, when style counts more than real accomplishment. We are impressed with outward appearances. We are easily distracted from unspectacular disciplines that lead to excellence. Life is skimmed from the surface. The depths remain largely unexplored.* [13]

I believe that in this brief paragraph Christenson has put his finger right on the problem and the myth. As important as love is, we need more than that. We need to build Christian character in our kids, and that takes time and discipline. "Just love" will not be enough, but love full of knowledge and wise insight will equip our kids with the Holy Spirit's power to live now and in the future.

Chapter Three Notes

1. Alvin Toffler, *Future Shock* (New York: Random House, Inc., 1970), p. 211.

2. Philippians 1:9 PHILLIPS.

3. *See* Tim Timmons, *Maximum Living in a Pressure Cooker World* (Waco: Word Publishing, 1979), p. 163.

4. Charles Swindoll, *Improving Your Serve* (Waco: Word Publishing, 1981), p. 125. Swindoll quotes these statistics from "The Battered Wife: What's Being Done?" *Los Angeles Times,* April 27, 1978.

5. John Naisbitt, *Megatrends: Ten New Directions Transforming Our Lives* (New York: Warner Books, Inc., 1982).

6. Toffler, *Future Shock,* p. 5.

7. Ibid., p. 23.

8. Alvin Toffler, *The Third Wave* (New York: William Morrow & Co., Inc., 1980), p. 185.

9. Naisbitt, *Megatrends,* p. 145.

10. Ibid., p. 40.

11. Eugene Kennedy, *Living With Everyday Problems* (Chicago: Thomas More Press, 1974), p. 9.

12. The six steps on problem solving are adapted from *The Universal Traveler* by Don Koberg and Jim Bograll (Los Altos, California: William Kaufmann, Inc., 1972). Another fine resource is the *Creativity Newsletter* by Anita Halstead, P.O. Box 1952, Lynnwood, Washington 98036.

13. Paul Anderson, *Building Christian Character* (Minneapolis: Bethany House Publishers, 1980), p. 7.

Part II
Do You Really Like Being a Dad?

That Is, Do You Actually *Like* Your Kids?

The next three chapters deal with tough questions. A lot of dads are looking for ways to improve, but they have never stopped to ask themselves if they really like their work. And fathering *is* work. It helps to *really like your kids*. And that's why we look at these questions:

Do you try to see them "real"? That is, do you accept your kids as they are or do you play the "if and when" game?

Are you willing to risk it? Fathering can be either a great adventure or something that lands somewhere between a real drag and "just playing it safe."

Four
Do You Try to See Them Real?
Love Never Has to Say "If" or "When"

Every day you should be seeing the world in a new personal way. The tree outside your house is no longer the same—so look at it. Your husband, wife, child, mother, father all are changing daily so look at them. Everything is in the process of change, including you.

Leo Buscaglia[1]

Faith, Hope and Love do not come in half sizes.

Postcard Received From Eight-Year-Old Boy

If I could change my mom and dad: I'd make them less rigid, make them listen to what I say before they answer, make it so they don't assume the worst all the time.

Girl, Age Eleven[2]

In N. Richard Nash's play *The Rainmaker*, Starbuck, the dreamer of dreams that almost never come true, complains to Lizzie about a world in which reality falls short of a man's vision.

STARBUCK   . . . Nothing's as pretty in your hands as it was in your head. There ain't no world near as good as the world I got up here *(angrily tapping his forehead).* Why?

LIZZIE   I don't know. Maybe it's because you don't take time to see it. Always on the go—here, there, nowhere. Running away . . . keeping your own company. Maybe if you'd keep company with the world . . .

STARBUCK   *(doubtfully)* I'd learn to love it?

LIZZIE   You might—if you saw it real. Some nights I'm in the kitchen washing the dishes. And Pop's playing poker with the boys. Well, I'll watch him real close. And at first, I'll just see an ordinary middle-aged man—not very interesting to look at. And then, minute by minute, I'll see little things I never saw in him before. Good things and bad things—queer little habits I never noticed he had—and ways of talking I never paid any mind to. And suddenly I know who he is—and I love him so much I could cry! And I want to thank God I took the time to see him *real.*[3]

Seeing Them Real Means Acceptance

I found the above lines by N. Richard Nash in a profound little devotional book called *Creative Brooding* by Robert Raines.[4] Lizzie's words, "I want to thank God I took the time to see him real," are directed at her father, of course, but their application is universal. Any father could take Lizzie's advice and start "seeing his family real," because when

What Kids Need Most in a Dad

you see someone real, you accept that person without passing all the usual judgments. What could be more important for a father to learn than that? The power of acceptance—of seeing and loving our children for who they are—reaches far beyond what we could ever imagine. The freedom we give our children to be who they are may well be the very basis of their self-esteem. Bruce Larson tells a beautiful story of the startling power of such acceptance:

> We had a thumb-sucker in our family who finally got to first grade and still sucked his thumb. I was frantic and tried everything I knew to break him of the habit, including scoldings, arguments, prayer with him, prayer for him, and the vile-tasting things that are concocted to put on children's thumbs to deter them from this persistent habit. But he was unable to stop. I kept telling him that I was doing all this for his own good and he heartily agreed!
>
> But one day I realized what my true motives were. I was really embarrassed to have my child advertising to the world the emotional needs of his own home and the inadequacy of his parents. I saw that my love for this child was conditioned by my need for him to stop this habit. When God showed me this, I made a new commitment of myself to Him and began to affirm what a truly wonderful son I had.
>
> I stopped correcting, nagging, or even referring to the thumb-sucking in any way. God had set me free and I secretly called my son by a new name, "Mr. Wonderful." I didn't care if he ever stopped sucking his thumb. The miracle is that in ten days he stopped cold and hasn't sucked his thumb since.[5]

Different Kinds of Love

This wonderful little peek into Bruce Larson's family circle shows far more than his transparency; it vividly illustrates the different kinds of love that people can show to one another.

There is the "I'll love you if and when . . ." kind of love. As Josh McDowell writes, this is:

> . . . the love you and I give or receive when certain requirements are met. You have to do something to earn it. . . . Parents often communicate this type of love by saying, in effect, to their children, "If you'll get good grades . . . if you'll choose a different set of friends . . . if you'll dress or act a certain way, you'll have our love."[6]

Another kind of conditional love is "I love you because. . . ." In this case, love is not based so much on performance as it is on attitudes or qualities. We may love our children because they are so cute, so cooperative, so bright—because we're so proud of them. The "because of" love and the "if and when" love are quite similar. Both come with strings attached—and our children know it.

Is there something about your son or daughter that is hard to live with? Most dads would have to answer, "Well, now that you mention it, yes, there is. I keep reminding him [or her] about it, but. . . ."

But what? I'm not suggesting we give up on discipline and training, but perhaps we need to blend our discipline with the kind of acceptance that allows us to call our kids Mr. or Miss Wonderful, to celebrate who they really are, *in spite of their imperfections or failures.* And when we can really do that—whole not halfheartedly—we will love them without the strings, without the conditions and requirements. This is the kind of love, writes Josh McDowell, that is:

> . . . *so startling and so beautiful that I wish everyone could bend his will to accept it. It is love without conditions.*
>
> *This love says, "I love you in spite of what you may be like deep down inside. I love you no matter what could change about you. You can't do anything to turn off my love. I love you, PERIOD!"*[7]

To see our children real, to accept them as they are, to love them, *period*—this is the most powerful kind of love we can demonstrate as parents. It is the very kind of love demonstrated by the heavenly Father whose "perfect love drives out fear . . ." (1 John 4:18 NIV).

Granted, our love for our children is far from perfect, but God gives the Christian parent the power of His Spirit. As we tap His resources, we can learn the subtle and difficult lessons of acceptance. And as we accept our children, we free them to be who they are in a world that is trying to tell them every day to be someone else.

How Do We Begin?

How do we begin to do this? How do we love our kids in real and tangible ways that say, "I really do accept you. I love you, *period!*" Following are a few ideas you may want to consider, but don't be limited to my thoughts. Love takes all kinds of shapes and forms. What is important is that you give it shape and form in your family.

1. *Use your eyes.* Take some time today to stop and see your kids for who they really are. Do you ever realize they are God's miracles, which He has given to you? People often

say to me, "I might believe in miracles if you could show me one." And I always reply, "Just come over to my house. I've got two of them: Zac and Josh. They eat potato chips and it turns into muscle!"

Another way to use your eyes to love your kids is to take time to look them right in the eye. Look in and see the person deep down inside struggling to get out.

In his fine book *How to Really Love Your Child,* Dr. Ross Campbell recalls the time his family moved to a new home. During the first days in the new place, his two boys, ages six and two at the time, started to get whiny, irritable, and underfoot in general. Dr. Campbell and his wife, who were trying to get the house in shape, got very irritated with the boys but decided that their behavior was being caused by the recent move. Then Campbell had an important insight:

> *One night I was thinking about my boys and I had the idea of imagining myself in their place. The answer to their behavioral problems suddenly hit me like a hammer. Pat and I were with the boys night and day and talked to them frequently. But we were so intent on the housework that we never really gave them their rightful attention, we never made eye contact and seldom made physical contact. Their emotional tanks had run dry, and* by their behavior *they were asking, "Do you love me?" In their childlike, normally irrational way, they were asking, "Do you love me now that we're in a new place? Are things still the same with us? Do you still love me?" So typical of children during a time of change.* [8]

Dr. Campbell and his wife immediately started giving their children extra attention—lots of holding and hugging and looking them right in the eye. The change was almost instantaneous. The boys soon became their happy, normal selves. In describing the importance of eye contact, Dr. Campbell says:

> *Eye contact is crucial not only in making good communicational contact with a child, but in filling his emotional needs. Without realizing it, we use eye contact as a primary means of conveying love, especially to children. The child uses eye contact with his parents (and others) to feed emotionally. The more parents make eye contact with their child as a means of expressing their love, the more a child is nourished with love and the fuller is his emotional tank.*

2. *Use your heart.* Love them for who they really are. Do you enjoy being their dad? Are you really, really glad that they're your kids? Have you taken time lately to thank God for these wonderful gifts you call your children? Or has life been so busy that you see them only as challenges, as mischiefs, as time eaters, as heavy responsibilities, or as headaches and problems?

If being a dad has become a bit of a drag, take some time to let God rearrange your priorities and touch your heart with gratitude and surprise.

3. *Use your ears.* It is worth repeating that God gave us two ears and one mouth and that should be indicative of the amount of time we spend listening versus the amount of time we spend speaking to our children. One of the greatest ways that we demonstrate our acceptance of our kids is by listening to them. Nothing lets them know how much we value them as much as remembering what they have said.

Eric Hoffer, the famed San Francisco dockworker and philosopher who has written so many best-selling books, tells of how he was given a special kind of acceptance by someone who listened. Hoffer inexplicably went blind at the age of seven and stayed that way until his eyesight miraculously returned at the age of fifteen. A Bavarian peasant woman cared for him and she is the one who taught him the power of listening and remembering.

This woman must have really loved me, because those eight years of blindness are in my mind as a happy time. I remember a lot of talk and laughter. I must have talked a great deal, because Martha used to say again and again, "I remember you said this. . . . You remember you said that. . . ." She remembered everything I said and all of my life I have had the feeling that what I think and what I say are worth remembering. She gave me that.[10]

4. *Use your mouth* to speak your acceptance and unconditional love. Despite all the emphasis of late on nonverbal communication, words are still one of the best ways to send a message. If we love our kids, we must tell them so. When was the last time you told your children that you accept them unconditionally, no matter how they do in class, on the athletic field, or in the school orchestra? Try sitting down with your children and asking them if they really understand what you mean when you say you accept them unconditionally, and that means you love them the same whether they do well or poorly. See if they can phrase the idea in their own words. Remember, it is not just the content of a message delivered but the content received that really counts. Encourage your children to give you feedback so that you know you're getting through.

Where the Angel Kissed Me

I heard a story some years ago about a teenager who had a very obvious birthmark over much of his face. And yet, it didn't seem to bother him. His self-esteem seemed secure. He related well with the other students and was well liked. He seemed to be in no way self-conscious about his very large birthmark, which was obvious to everyone else.

Finally, someone asked how this could be. "Are you aware of the fact that you have this large birthmark on your face?"

He replied, "Of course I am."

"Can you tell me, then, why it does not seem to bother you in the slightest?"

The young man smiled and said, "When I was very young, my father started telling me that birthmark was there for two reasons: one, it was where the angel kissed me; two, the angel had done that so my father could always find me easily in a crowd."

He then continued, "My dad told me this so many times with so much love that as I grew up, I actually began to feel sorry for the other kids who weren't kissed by the angel like I was."

Words are such a powerful tool. They can encourage or discourage, accept or deny, create hope or depression. Are you realizing the power of words in your own home? How much time do you actually spend talking *with* (not *to*) your kids each week?

5. *Use your hands* to touch your kids with love. Studies have indicated that children can actually grow up thwarted and stunted from the lack of touch. In our home, probably one of the most profound things that I do with my boys is wrestle with them. I heard somewhere that each child needs a bare minimum of eight hugs a day just to stay healthy. A child needs twelve to fifteen hugs, or more, a day if you

really want him to blossom. I'm not sure how such statistics were measured, but it does give us a hint as to how much acceptance we can convey through the awesome power of human touch. Our bodies may be one of the finest tools that God has given us for developing genuine intimacy with those around us.

6. *Use your feet* to convey your acceptance. Do you attend your kids' ball games? Do you run and play with them in the backyard? When was the last time you just went for a walk with one of your kids? Do you spend some *individual* time with each of your kids, each week? Do you pull them aside and give them some focused attention to help them realize that they're different from their brothers and sisters and that you think that's okay?

Charlie Shedd, who has probably written as many books on marriage and the family as anyone I know, says that he has done three things for his family that have held it together.

First, he makes sure that he takes his wife out to dinner alone once a week.

Second, he spends fifteen minutes a day talking with his wife. He's one of those people who really does believe that the best thing he can do for his kids is to love his wife. This is a time to talk about feelings, not about business.

The third thing he does, he says, is to spend some special time each month with *each* of his kids. He does it by taking each of his kids out to dinner alone once a month, and he indicates that even during those difficult adolescent years when most kids want to cut off communication, his kids still not only accepted his invitation for dinner but relished it as well.

Use All Your Tools—Often

God has given us some wonderful tools for accepting our kids. He's given us eyes to see them differently. He's given us hearts to love them deeply. He's given us ears to listen carefully to their needs. He's given us mouths to share our love and acceptance in words. He's given us hands to hug and touch our kids and let them know in those countless nonverbal ways how much we love them. And finally, He's given us feet to walk alongside our children on their long journey of growing up.

In a book called *The Self in Pilgrimage,* Earl Loomis, Jr., tells an amazing story about Emperor Frederick, who ruled the Roman Empire in the thirteenth century. The emperor, it seems, wanted to conduct a controlled experiment with the young children of slaves in order to figure out what language Adam and Eve spoke in the Garden of Eden. According to his logic, if the children never heard a human voice, then the language they would eventually speak would be the same as that of Adam and Eve. (This is admittedly fairly primitive logic, but then you must remember it was the thirteenth century.)

In order to insure that none of the children would ever hear the sound of a human voice, the wet nurses in charge of the children were given strict orders to maintain complete silence while caring for them. The children were given the best of food, warmth, and the like. But they never heard any spoken words and the implication is that they were also given a minimum of touch or any other kind of communication, for that matter.

In concluding the story, Loomis writes:

> *It is tremendously difficult for a woman to be silent with a child. Nonetheless, the nurses succeeded. According to the account, not one of them uttered*

*a single word to any of the children. In other words,
the experimental conditions were a success. But
the children all died.*[11]

What a tragic and powerful story. Dads, don't forget
those wonderful tools God gave you. Use all of them often
with your kids.

Chapter Four Notes

1. Leo Buscaglia, *Love* (New York: Fawcett Book Group, 1982), p. 41.

2. Erwin Lutzer, *If I Could Change My Mom and Dad* (Chappaqua, New York: Christian Herald, 1982), p. 58.

3. N. Richard Nash, *The Rainmaker* (New York: Random House, Inc., 1954).

4. Robert A. Raines, *Creative Brooding* (New York: Macmillan Publishing Co., Inc., 1966), p. 105.

5. Bruce Larson, *Dare to Live Now* (Grand Rapids: Zondervan Publishing House, 1965), p. 28.

6. Josh McDowell, *Givers, Takers, and Other Kinds of Lovers* (Wheaton, Illinois: Tyndale House Publishers, 1980), p. 38.

7. Ibid., p. 43.

8. Dr. Ross Campbell, *How to Really Love Your Child* (Wheaton, Illinois: Victor Books, 1977), p. 43.

9. Ibid., p. 37.

10. Quoted by Alan Loy McGinnis in *The Friendship Factor* (Minneapolis: Augsburg Publishing House, 1979), p. 104.

11. Earl A. Loomis, Jr., *The Self in Pilgrimage* (New York: Harper & Row Publishers, Inc., 1960), p. 54.

Five
Are You Willing to Risk It?
The Adventure of Fathering

You can live on bland food so as to avoid an ulcer: drink no tea or coffee or other stimulants, in the name of health: go to bed early and stay away from night life: avoid all controversial subjects so as never to give offense: mind your own business and avoid involvement in other people's problems: spend money only on necessities and save all you can. You can still break your neck in the bathtub, and it will serve you right.

Eileen Guder[1]

Life is either a daring adventure or nothing at all.

Helen Keller

My father and I have a good relationship. It's easy to tell him my problems without him getting mad. The only thing wrong I think is that he always is in a right position. Even if he's wrong, he still is right. I guess that fathers should be right, but I think they should admit that they're wrong if they're wrong.

Chris, Teenage Boy

Being a father is not only one of the greatest privileges on earth; it can also be one of the greatest adventures that I can ever know. But, if I'm not careful, I can miss it either because of lack of effort or lack of awareness. It is so easy to get caught up in the daily routines of living the good life. It is so easy to miss the wonder and fullness and joy that fatherhood can bring.

We all hear constantly about the crisis facing the family, and it's true. Today's families face some of the greatest challenges and dangers in history. But I also like to believe that in those challenges and dangers lie great opportunities for adventure, if we stay awake and aware of what is happening.

"Living the good life," wrote Nikolai Berdyaev, "is frequently dull and flat and commonplace. Our greatest problem," he claimed, "is to make it fiery and creative and capable of spiritual struggle."

Because we live in a "good life society" we can easily be sucked into an existence where the greatest excitement in life is sitting home on weekends watching the "Late Night Special," or perhaps finally finding a deodorant that lasts twelve hours. The irony—and the tragedy—of our society is that it *appears* that one doesn't have to risk anymore. Without too much effort, in our society you can live an entire lifetime without getting really hungry, really thirsty, really cold, really hot, or really challenged. And the sad part is that all too often—usually when it's too late—we discover that we haven't lived our lives to the fullest.

The increasing pace of life in our society demands so much of our time that we often fall into that subtle trap of just existing, just going through the motions with our families. Without realizing it, we choose to believe that life is boring. Without realizing it, our lives begin to fulfill our uninspired expectations. Our highly developed media have convinced us to surround ourselves with things—material expressions of success. But again, the paradox is that these things tend to insulate us from the life that could be more adventurous. The padding, around our waists and our lives, gets a little thicker each year and our excitement for life slowly erodes.

Little do we realize how powerfully these attitudes affect our children. Our kids need large doses of adventure in order to change, discover, and grow. If they aren't sufficiently challenged by real-life adventures, they will seek and find other fictitious adventures of significantly less value. I'm not surprised when I see youth exploring drugs, premarital sex, or other delinquent behavior. I don't condone any of this; I'm simply not surprised. Kids are conducting their own experiments and using their bodies and souls as test tubes. Why? Often it is simply their way of seeking their own idea of newness and adventure. It is their means of breaking what Paul Tournier calls, ". . . the deadly monotony of a society which to them has become overorganized, fossilized and impotent."[2]

But I am surprised that Christian fathers who claim the life-changing message of Jesus Christ aren't on the edge of adventure more often. I've seen all too many fathers withdraw behind the walls of niceness, apathy, and boredom. Without realizing it, our everyday lives come to depend on cars, cosmetics, and credit cards. Few dads realize that they are atrophying mentally as well as physically. It is easy to fall prey to status, security, conformity, and comfort. We've become a society more concerned with how we *look* rather than *what we see.*

The best way I know to bring new adventure and exuberance into our daily existence is by daring to risk, daring to grow, daring to let go of some of those attachments we have allowed to limit us for so long. There are three things to remember about daring to risk and seeking to grow:

- Risk and growth are worth it.
- It is not as difficult as we think.
- It is never too late to start.

But before we start, perhaps we need to ask ourselves if daring to risk *is* really worth it. What is the bottom line? What will be the results?

Risk Enlivens Us

One danger in living the "safe" life is that we keep putting things off. As Tournier says, "Most people spend their entire lives indefinitely preparing to live."[3] The good-life mentality has us looking forward to that vacation in Hawaii next year—or maybe two years from now. We tend to put off our adventures by thinking that an adventure has to be a big project, some kind of major operation. The result is that we dissolve our appreciation for the magical moments that surround us now. In our constant striving for big moments, we overlook the beauty of the little ones. And we forget that, in reality, that's all we have—the moments, the little pockets of time that are crammed with all of life's delicious possibilities. William Blake's encouragement in his poem "Auguries of Innocence" to see the world in a grain of sand still remains a beautiful challenge. We don't see *with* our eyes as much as we see *through* them. We see the world according to who we are. If I see life as something that is always "going to happen later," I will miss it. If I'm not willing to risk it, to go for it without worrying about all the details or all of the problems, I simply wind up procrastinating over the joy of being alive.

Risk Deepens Our Lives

A friend of mine said to me recently, "It's not how far you go in life, but how deep you go that really counts." No one epitomized this more than Helen Keller. Though struck totally blind and deaf from an undiagnosed disease at the age of nineteen months, she refused to give in to the circumstances. Trapped inside of herself, she struggled through the barriers of silence to become free. The evidence of her difficulty, pain, struggle, and willingness to risk the best has touched all of our lives.

Some years ago, a friend of mine and I decided to explore what Helen Keller's world might be like. I bandaged my eyes and taped them so I was totally blind. (People who asked were told that I had injured my eyes in an industrial accident.) For almost a week, I had to rely on my other senses, which I soon discovered I had allowed to atrophy somewhat from lack of use.

I can vividly remember the fresh joy of learning and growing as I groped in the dark. My friend Dick Horton encouraged me to explore my abilities by putting me in circumstances that demanded risk. He had me jump, for example, off a twenty-five-foot tower into a lake. I remember feeling as though it took at least half an hour to hit the icy water. But the joy was beyond anything I had ever imagined. Even the simple tasks of eating and trying to write a letter to my family became genuine adventures. All the difficulties and delicate joys of being alive were enhanced beyond measure by my temporary "blindness."

We may not want to try exactly the same blindfold experiment with our kids—it would probably be impractical in most cases. But isn't it possible that we could create certain controlled-risk situations to help our children learn the equalities that we want so much to teach them? Isn't it possible that you and I could begin making our family times real adventures? Limiting one of our senses is only one of many possibilities.

I know that one of the qualities I want to instill in my children, more than any other, is the quality of courage. I believe that courage is the price of admission to life at its deepest levels. The word *courage* stems from a French root, *coeur,* meaning "heart." And just as one's heart keeps the body alive by pumping blood to the arms, legs, and brain, so courage gives substance and impetus to life. Along with faith, it is a genuine antidote to fear, which explains in part the numerous scriptural admonitions to be strong, to have good courage, to fear not. (For example, read Joshua 1:6, 7, 9; 1 Kings 2:2; 2 Chronicles 15:7; and Isaiah 35:4.)

And yet, how will my children learn of courage and strength? How will they learn genuine faith, confidence, and trust? How will they learn how to risk and grow, if I do not share these kinds of experiences with them and model that kind of behavior for them?

All evidence indicates that there can be no growth without risk. There can be no change without taking a chance. And there's no real sense of aliveness without a sense of daring.

I want my boys to become strong, biblical men. But theology can't live in a vacuum. God's incredible promises remain latent until we risk claiming them and living them out. My experiment with blindness was a kind of parable that taught me again about how the Christian's life of faith is difficult and subtle—and far more exciting than we usually imagine. Paul, who knew something about faith and courage and being strong through God, said it perfectly when he wrote to the Ephesians, "Now to him who by his power within us is able to do infinitely more than we ever dare to ask or imagine—to Him be glory in the Church and in Christ Jesus for ever and ever, amen!" (Ephesians 3:20, 21 PHILLIPS).

Risk Enlarges Our Horizons

Sister Corita, the famed Catholic nun who invested her life in the creative arts, said, "There are no rules for leaping into the new, because no one has ever been there before."

Every time we risk, we expand our horizons. Every time we involve our family in an area of adventure, we increase their capacity for growth and we widen and deepen their hopes for a stronger future.

One of the saddest and most subtle consequences of not risking is that you stay where you are. To risk is to move beyond your previous conception of who you are. Risking expands your experience of life, your experience of self, and above all, your experience of God.

As we read the New Testament, we see men and women whose lives were full of uncertainty. Excitement abounded. Social pressure—and often social censure—were the order of the day. There were mass conversions, sudden outbursts of faith, and equally sudden times of danger and difficulty. There was, however, absolutely no boredom. Christianity did not get dull until later, when the church began to water down the strong flavor of the Gospel with the prudence and caution of the worldly. And this viewpoint is still with us to this day—a safe, careful, sensible approach that takes no chances and runs no risks.

Several years ago, a study of teenagers revealed that most would rather settle for low success than to aim high and risk failure. I am hoping, praying, and working to help my children grow to be teenagers and young men who are willing to risk reaching for the heights rather than be content with the mediocre. In our home, you will often hear, "Those who say they *can* and those who say they *can't*— are usually both right." I know, however, that my children will learn more by experience than they will by mere slogans. I want to be the kind of father who can not only encourage my children to risk more in life but who can be a proper model of how to go about it as well.

There's an ancient proverb that says, "I heard and I forgot; I saw and I remembered; I did and I understood." The spirit of adventure and risking is usually more "caught" than taught. Having both boys join me on a wilderness expedition had to increase their confidence for meeting unknown situations. Showing my oldest son how to catch a fish with his bare hands may have an effect that reaches far beyond that single experience. Being with them in new situations teaches them that trying new things (and even failing) is worth the risk.

What Kind of Risks Should We Take?

We have looked at why "risking it" can be worth it. Perhaps we also need to consider *what kind* of risks would be worth it. I'm not against living in a sane manner and according to normal rules of safety. I'm not in favor of teaching our kids how to play Chicken or Russian Roulette, but life provides all kinds of opportunities to take legitimate—even necessary—risks.

Management expert Peter Drucker once said there are essentially four kinds of risks that one can take.

1. The risk one must accept.
2. The risk one can afford to take.
3. The risk one cannot afford to take.
4. The risk one cannot afford not to take.[4]

For me, a Christian father, *the risk that I must accept* is that of being more involved in my children's lives in a way that invites them into the joyful adventure of being fully alive. To be fully alive means to know God. Our God is a God of great adventure. The Exodus is referred to more times in the Psalms than any other event. We need to remember that we are now and always will be a part of God's "New Exodus." Christianity is more than just a good start. God is more than just a good idea. The Christian life is a long, harrowing and often hilarious journey. I want my children to be a part of that with me.

The key is time. *I must spend time with my children.* There is no substitute, no alternative, no excuse. I either spend the time or I do not accept the risk that automatically became mine when I became a father.

We will look more at the element of time in chapter 9, but right here note that one of your best investments of time is to do something adventurous with your kids that has Christian overtones or connections. Camping, for example, is a natural. Every summer Summit Expedition offers 5 special wilderness experiences for dads and their children. To most of them—parent and child—it is one of the most exciting things they have ever done. To me, however, the most exciting thing about it is tying the life of adventure to the Christian faith.

And what about *the risks that we can afford to take?* There are not only many different kinds of adventures but there are many different levels of adventure as well. Some are very easy because of circumstances, personality, or abilities. Some risks are more difficult. For some, meeting new people is done with medium discomfort, while others die a thousand deaths before every encounter. Some have the ability to stand up in front of an audience and talk with little or no effort. Statistics show, however, that for most people, public speaking is one of the most frightening things imaginable.

What then are the risks that we can afford to take with our children? I think one essential risk is helping our children be the very best version of who they can be. This doesn't mean that I am to play the taskmaster or the driving kind of coach who is always raising the bar another inch. What it does mean is that I must take numerous small risks to demonstrate to my children what it means to be the best you can be as you go about the "dailyness" of life.

For example, I'd like my children to know how to stay curious amidst the boredom that seems to have invaded most of our schools. So, I have to continually demonstrate my curiosity about life and learning new things.

I also hope they will be able to risk celebration amid the mundane routines of life and I certainly want them to risk openness in the midst of a world that tends to scorn honesty or take advantage of it. And so again, I have to model that and celebrate the wonders of the ordinary. I have to model being open and transparent and that might even mean admitting to my children that I am not perfect, that I am afraid sometimes, that I do make mistakes and am not always sure what the right answer really is.

And I'm glad Peter Drucker was insightful enough to remind us that there are *risks that we cannot afford to take.* As I've already pointed out, there is very little value in risking for the sake of risking. When I talk about "risking it" I don't mean teaching our kids to have lots of machismo. And there is even less value in risking simply to gain attention, or to justify our compulsions.

For example, what about the way you drive the car—especially when your kids are with you? We teach our children a great deal in the way we operate an automobile, particularly when we are dashing to church on Sunday morning, already fifteen minutes late.

What about seat belts? Do you teach your kids to "buckle up" or do you all just "risk it"? Like you, I do not have a perfect record in buckling up. But I try to remember it and to show my children that some risks just aren't worth it.

My boys, for example, are very sensitive to motorcycle riders who aren't wearing helmets. Every time we see a biker on the road without a helmet, my boys comment, "That's not right, is it, Daddy?" I heartily agree and then I try to remember to wear my own helmet when I go out riding my ten-speed.

There are many ways to teach our children about risks they cannot afford to take. Perhaps the greatest risk we fathers cannot afford to take is to *not* teach them these things.

Finally, Drucker says there are *risks we cannot afford not to accept.* It is a myth to think that if we can only stay where we are, then we'll be happy. We need to recognize that in our families, our love is either growing or dying. There is no in-between. We must continue to grow or else we fall into the saddest trap of all: the so-called life of mere existence. Laura Bennett, one of our Summit Expedition instructors, said it so well: "The risk of not risking is simply too great a risk for me to take."

Courage Comes in Three Parts

Like most fathers, I want my children to be joyful. But I know to be truly joyous means having the ability and desire to take risks. I have mentioned the importance of courage, but just how does a child (or an adult) learn to be courageous? Part of the answer has to lie in three critical areas:

1. *Decisions.* What our children will become will largely depend on the decisions and choices they make. Decisions take courage. It takes courage to make a decision and it takes courage to accept the consequences of that decision.

2. *Commitments.* It takes courage to be an individual—to stand alone if necessary, not only for what is right but for one's own personal integrity as well. Choosing what is right amid the confusion, conflict, and complexities of our day can be a baffling and frightening task. Sticking to commitments is especially tough for our children because the pressure from their peer group is so strong. In fact, your child's efforts to be who he or she really is may be the very basis of all other forms of courage.

3. *Caring.* Ours is an age of incredible apathy and indifference. I want my children to gain the courage to be involved in the needs of the world around them. They can learn how to make decisions; they can become dedicated and committed; but if they fail to care, it will all be so much noise and wind.

Decisions, commitments, caring—they all begin in our families and they all require that we, the parents, model real courage and a real spirit of adventure for our children, who are watching us so very carefully.

Can You Know if You're Happy?

This time called life is far more sacred and special than any of us could ever imagine. Our task, or should I say our privilege, is to become more aware of the specialness of life and to participate in it as deeply and as fully as we can. Nothing is as precious as the experience of living in touch with yourself, with others, and with God. I want my children to not only be able to talk about God but to also be able to know Him personally and experientially. There is no other way to true joy. I don't want my children to grow up with a watercolor kind of happiness that washes off in the first rain. I want to know real and lasting joy.

In our society, it's so easy to seek Band-Aids rather than true adventure and end up with a kind of sterilized unhappiness that we label "contentment." If we fail to take risks and continue to only play it safe, we simply lock ourselves into a false and insulated kind of security that in difficult times only pushes us further into those dislocated and empty pockets of uneasiness where we are not sure whether or not we are really happy.

I believe we can know true joy. We can experience the worthwhileness and adventure of being alive. Being willing to risk in areas of decision, commitment, and caring are ways to start making the changes that lead to true joy. Are you willing to risk it, Dad? If so you should find, as I did, encouragement in these fine words quoted by Leo Buscaglia:

To laugh is to risk appearing the fool.
To weep is to risk appearing sentimental.
To reach out to others is to risk getting involved.
To show your feelings is to risk exposing your humanity.
To place your ideas and dreams before the crowd is to risk their loss.
To love is to risk not being loved in return.
To hope is to risk pain.
To try is to risk failure.

But risk must be taken, because the greatest hazard in life is to risk *nothing.* The person who risks nothing does nothing, has nothing, and is nothing. He may avoid suffering and sorrow, but he simply cannot learn, feel, change, grow, live, or love.

Only the person who risks is free.[6]

Chapter Five Notes

1. Eileen Guder, *God, But I'm Bored!* (New York: Doubleday & Co., Inc., 1971), p. 53.

2. Paul Tournier, *The Adventure of Living* (New York: Harper & Row Publishers, Inc., 1976), pp. 6, 7.

3. Ibid., p. 117.

4. Peter Drucker, *Managing for Results* (New York: Harper & Row Publishers, Inc., 1964), p. 206.

5. For more information send to Summit Expedition, P.O. Box 521, San Dimas, California 91773.

6. Leo Buscaglia, *Living, Loving, and Learning* (Thorofare, New Jersey: Charles B. Slack, Inc., 1982), p. 262-264.

Part III
Do You Know How to Be a Better Dad?

Everyone Needs All the Help They Can Get

These final four chapters are designed to be a "toolbox" of ideas and suggestions to help you with the task of fathering. Every father knows that he can never get enough of these tools to help him in his never-ending responsibilities to construct, maintain, and at times repair his kids.

First we'll look at the whole idea of planning. Do you have a plan, Dad? (A lot of fathers don't seem to have a clue.) Do you know how to set goals? Do you know the difference between a purpose and a goal? Most of all, do you know how to reach a goal once you set it?

Next comes the "Alphabet of Fathering": two chapters of rapid-fire ideas and suggestions for things you can actually do as well as many things to remember as you work with your children. The Alphabet contains everything from games to strategies for knowing how to talk to your children, how to discipline them, and how to use the word *no* as well as the word *yes*. The Alphabet gives you practical ideas that you can use with your kids —starting now.

Finally, you will examine three critical ingredients for fathering: time, consistency, and enthusiam. Being a father means many things, but what kids need most in a dad is the fire and zeal that come from a heart full of love that translates into action.

What Kids Need Most in a Dad

Six
Do You Have a Plan?
Some Dads Don't Even Have a Clue

Goals—everyone has them, though not everyone is able to state what they are. In one sense, to have no goal is a goal in itself . . . if managing your time is managing your life, and if our calendar should reflect who and what we truly value, most of us would have to admit we're not doing a very good job with our families.

Edward Dayton[1]

It is not the critic who counts: not the man who points out how the strong man stumbled or where the doer of deeds could have done them better. The credit belongs to the man who is actually in the arena; whose face is marred by the dust and sweat . . . far better it is to dare mighty things, to win glorious triumphs even though checkered by failure, than to rank with those poor spirits who neither enjoy nor suffer much because they live in the gray twilight that knows neither victory nor defeat.

Theodore Roosevelt[2]

A father is someone who helps you plan out your life, who helps you be the best person that you could be. A father is a leader. A father is love expressed in little things like having dinner with you, spending time with you, giving you encouragement and direction. A father is not someone who runs away from life when things get tough but helps you hang on and know where to take the next step.

Kathy, Age Sixteen

I can identify strongly with the feelings of the man who wrote:

The objective of all dedicated fathers shall be to thoroughly analyze all problems prior to their occurrence, have answers to all these problems, and move swiftly to solve these problems when called upon. However . . . when you're up to your hips in alligators, it is sometimes very difficult to remind yourself that your main objective was to drain the swamp!

Fathering is like that in a lot of ways. We feel pushed and shoved in so many different directions that sometimes it is hard to remember who we are much less what we're here for. Overwhelmed by braces and flu bugs, bills that never seem to end, clothes which either don't fit anymore or just aren't "cool," it's sometimes hard just to keep up much less stay ahead. Everywhere we turn there are more and more demands. The lists and expectations seem to go on endlessly.

So, when someone tells me that I should have better plans for my family, I sometimes feel as if I don't want to hear it. And yet, you're probably like me, in the sense of believing that my family is my highest priority and my hopes for my children are second to none.

In previous chapters, we have seen that fathering is more involved, more intricate, more complex, and sometimes more difficult than we allow ourselves to imagine. If that is true, then we dare not underestimate the value of planning.

In Part I we analyzed several myths that can hamper or mislead fathers. In this chapter on planning we are trying to counter still another fallacy: the myth of good intentions. To get specific about my goals and plans has a way of exposing all those wonderful platitudes, overgeneralizations, and bromides that I like to substitute for the plain, hard work that is inevitably involved in being a quality father.

Some years ago, I saw a book entitled *If You Don't Know Where You're Going, You'll Probably End Up Somewhere Else.*[3] Although it had nothing to do with fathering per se, it would make a great title for us dads—for I'm amazed at how many dads, including myself, consider fathering our most important priority and yet never stop long enough to set goals and to make real plans for the future. Somehow we expect these wonderful things that we dream of for our kids to happen through osmosis—or magic.

Some Tough Questions for Goal Setters

Consider, for example, the following questions:

1. What character qualities do you want your children to have by the time they're twenty-one years old? How do you plan to *insure* that they have them?
2. What are the three most important rules for your children? If they were asked the same question, would they come up with the same answers as you?
3. How are your kids different? What are you doing to provide for and even enhance their differences?
4. If someone were to ask your children, "What's really important in your family?" how would they answer?
5. *In the past two weeks,* what *specifically* did you do with your children to influence their

character, improve their skills, or shape their attitudes?

These are just a few of the many questions that we need to be asking ourselves and our families. As Paul said so well in his letter to the Ephesians:

Live life, then, with a due sense of responsibility, not as men who do not know the meaning of life but as those who do. *Make the best use of your time, despite all the evils of these days. Don't be vague but grasp firmly what you know to be the will of the Lord.*
Ephesians 5:15–17 PHILLIPS

Some things haven't changed since Paul penned those lines to the Ephesian Christians. We still face difficult days, but he gives us three solid principles to use with our families.

Accept Your Full Responsibility

I think Paul's advice to "live life, then, with a due sense of responsibility" was particularly designed for dads. One of the first steps is to learn how to be a father *on purpose.* I must realize the meaning and importance of my role as an intentional father. I simply can't ignore it or rationalize it away.

It is too easy to underestimate the influence that we fathers have on our kids—*positive or negative.* But I have an irreplaceable role as father to my children. I may be able to delegate a lot of my responsibilities at work, but I can never delegate my responsibilities as a father.

I've heard the following story many times and I'm sure you have, too. It seems there was a golfer who took a huge swing but missed the ball and only managed to take up a lot of dirt and a few hundred ants as well. He swung again, only to miss and again take up more huge gobs of dirt and

What Kids Need Most in a Dad

hundreds of ants. Finally, one ant looked over to another and said, "You know, if we want to get out of here alive, we'd better get on the ball!"

I've had plenty of days when I felt like one of those ants. I knew I had to get on the ball but sometimes I wasn't even sure where the ball was! It's on days like that that I have to go back to the basics. I have to accept my responsibility. I have to be deliberate and persistent even on those days when nothing seems to work. In short, I have to hang in there.

Someone said the difference between success and failure is that ability to hang in there five minutes longer. All of us know the tendency to want to quit too soon. We suffer guilt and depression about not being good enough or consistent enough or strong enough. One of the best things I ever read about guilt was the simple statement, "No one benefits from your feeling guilty."[4] I think that is especially true for fathers. Success is 90 percent perspiration and 10 percent inspiration. All of us have those days when we feel like miserable failures. In those situations, I encourage you to try a simple little acronym that we sometimes use in our Summit Expedition survival training:

STOP
THINK
OBSERVE
PLAN

When the responsibilities get a little too heavy, it never hurts to just simply stop and think. Observe what is going on and why things aren't working. And then make some plans to turn things around.

What Kids Need Most in a Dad

Make the Best Use of Your Time

Was Paul a time management specialist? Would he have worked in well as a high-powered executive in one of today's corporations? We might debate those questions, but we can't argue with the wisdom of what he says in Ephesians 5:16: "Make the best use of your time, despite all the evils of these days" (PHILLIPS). It's ironic how many dads try to apply this verse at the office but somehow forget to use it at home. Out on the job fathers use memos, charts, calendar books, and so on to make the best use of their time. But the minute they walk in the door at home, they seem to be unaware of the need to use time management skills for greater effectiveness.

And yet, a man's children are infinitely more sensitive and complex than any computer he might work with at the office. We talk a lot about pressure on the job, tension at the office, and so forth. What about pressure and tension at home? What are the pressures that are squeezing your children? Do they have time to tell you about them? Have you planned any time for your children? Half the time management books tell us again and again, *"Fail to plan, plan to fail."*

There's nothing really mysterious or magical about planning. Planning is simply the arrow which points in the direction of our future. Which direction do you want to go? Planning is simply trying to discover what you want to accomplish and how you hope to do that—before you commit yourself. Planning is simply moving from now into the future, from the way things are into the way we want things to be. It is simply trying to discover and understand and respond to what God's will and hopes are for your particular family.

A book I highly recommend that you read to be a better dad or a better manager is *Strategy for Living* by Edward

What Kids Need Most in a Dad

Dayton and Ted Engstrom. In the first chapter Dayton and Engstrom remind us, "How we live our life is determined by our GOALS. What goals we choose are determined by our PRIORITIES. Whether we reach our goals is determined by our PLANNING."[5] The authors spend the rest of the book explaining how to develop a creative "strategy for living," which is a process of integrating goals, priorities, and planning into the best life possible for each of us.

If you analyze what Dayton and Engstrom are saying concerning goals, priorities, and planning, you can see that a strategy for living starts with priorities. The key to using your time effectively is to know what your priorities are. The next step is to know what you want to get done—the setting of some specific goals. After that, you make your plans to reach those goals. Paul is right. These are difficult days, but time is the most precious possession we'll ever have and we must make good use of it. As I plan the use of my own time, I try to keep three principles in mind:

1. *We all have the same amount of time.* No one has any more or any less time than you or I do. Each day, each of us is given 1,440 minutes to use any way we wish. How I use those 1,440 minutes a day or 168 hours a week depends on my priorities. I try to "maximize my strengths" (that is, do what I do best) as I remember that the key to working with my family is to be effective if not always completely efficient. I never want to become a time nut, but I do try to establish clear priorities and goals.

2. *I use goals to know what I want to accomplish.* I try to establish long-range goals, mid-range goals, and short-term goals. Whenever possible I try to include Pam and the children in setting goals. Howard Hendricks says that he spends one day per month with his wife for primarily a time of planning how they can maximize their marriage and

What Kids Need Most in a Dad

their family. Pam and I have not gotten away every month to do this, but we have tried it with great benefit. When was the last time you and your wife took a day off, got away from the house, and just planned the future of your family?

3. *I try to put my goals in writing.* There is a distinct difference between a purpose and a goal. In general, purpose is the direction in which to move, but it is hard to measure. For example, my purpose might be to become a "dedicated Christian father." If I'm going to fulfill that purpose I need some goals that are accomplishable and measurable. They have to be measured by what needs to be done, and a date has to be set as to when I want to complete the task. For example, which of the following statements do you believe is a purpose? Which is a goal?

1. Spend more time with my family.
2. Read one book per month.
3. Read the Bible regularly.
4. Spend at least ten minutes per day praying for members of my family.
5. Do more outdoor things with my children.
6. Take a thirty-mile bike trip with my two sons by the end of the month.

For the record, all of the odd-numbered statements above are purposes and all of the even-numbered ones are goals. As you can see, the purposes are stated rather generally while the goals are much more specific and definite.[6]

Once you have your goals written down, keep them handy, either in your date book or posted somewhere on the wall in your study. Time management specialists estimate that fewer than 13 percent of us bother to write down our goals. To write down our goals keeps life in sharper focus, and that brings us to the third principle in Paul's advice to the Ephesians—which is also excellent advice for us.

Don't Be Vague

I have always admired Paul's logical thinking. First he reminds me to accept my responsibilities. Then I am to remember to make the best use of my time. Finally, I am not to be fuzzy-headed but am to grasp what I know to be the will of the Lord (Ephesians 5:17 PHILLIPS).

One of my biggest tendencies as a dad is to speak and operate in generalities. This is particularly easy to do when dealing with my children. For example, I tend to simply encourage my kids to "be honest" without ever giving them a definition of what honesty means and how it works out in practical ways in our lives. I am afraid I know a lot of other parents who teach values to their kids in the same general way. We tell them to be honest, truthful, kind, and loving without talking about—and modeling—specific ways to pull it off.

All this came home to me much more clearly not too long ago when Paul Lewis of Dad's Only asked me to write an article on how to instill courage in children. I said, "No problem, because to me, courage is one of the most important attributes that I want my kids to learn."

But I soon realized in attempting to put that article into print that teaching a quality such as courage is more complicated than I thought. Writing that article forced me to:

1. Understand my purpose clearly.
2. Develop some clear goals.
3. Break those goals down into specific concrete exercises that my children could experience.

First I decided to clearly state my purpose: to have my children understand and experience the quality of courage. Next I decided to set three measurable goals. The first was to work with my children to define the word *courage* in terms they could understand. I did just that by spending a lot of time with Zac and Josh talking about what courage meant from their viewpoint. They came up with definitions like "being brave" and "not being afraid."

My second goal was to make courage a regular topic of discussion (at least three times a week at dinner or bedtime) for two weeks. As we had these discussions, it became clear to all of us that courage wasn't just something that we needed while participating in sports or sleeping alone in dark rooms. We also need courage for making decisions and commitments, and we need courage when it comes to caring for one another and for other people in our very needy world.

My third goal was the development of some specific experiences that would require courage on the part of my sons. I wanted them to understand what courage meant from an experiential level. So, I set about creating some specific activities and exercises.

We decided to set up some controlled situations with a certain amount of physical risk. First we did simple things like trying to do as many push-ups as possible or trying to run all the way around our large block without stopping. Next we developed a little ramp in our backyard from which the boys could make exciting (to them) but safe jumps on their bikes. Zac and Josh loved the bike jump, and it gave us great opportunities to talk about courage and other related qualities such as safety. This involved checking the ramp to be sure it was solid, and so on.

Next we tried getting some boxing gloves and having the neighborhood kids come in and go a few rounds. In a situation like that, courage is no longer a vague idea but a very specific attitude.

Finally, late one Saturday afternoon we had Mom drop us

off a distance from home. Our assignment was to find our way home before dark. We had a great time together as we hiked back. I let the boys do as much of the "finding" of the correct streets as possible. At dinner that evening we had a special time as the boys shared with Mom what they had learned.

Stay in the Arena

There are so many things we fathers want to teach our children:

- To be better leaders.
- To have stronger self-esteem.
- To know how to solve problems more creatively.
- To learn responsible work and health habits.
- To know how to cope with guilt.
- To know how to enjoy life more.

The list is practically endless, but notice that the above statements are all in the category of purposes. In order to go beyond vague generalities we need to develop concrete goals and very real activities and exercises that are specific and measurable.

All of this sounds like a lot of fuss, and sometimes it is. But once I get into the specific goals and activities, then comes the best part—I get to do all of this with my children. At this point, fathering becomes a privilege and a joy.

In the next two chapters, we'll be looking at a storehouse of practical ways to guide, train, and just enjoy our kids. But before going on, a word of caution. In a book like this it's easy to soar into the stratosphere of idealism (which I have done on more than a few pages). Keep in mind, however, that ideals are great but we don't have to realize all of them in a day, a month, or even a year. All of these thoughts and ideas are simply a resource bank from which you can draw at your own pace. Use what you can and be satisfied with the little victories. Never forget that the process is as important as the goal. Being a father (as well as a child) is a journey, not a race. Give yourself a pat on the back frequently. Give yourself credit for being a dad who cares.

And don't expect to bat 1.000. Ted Williams won many major league batting crowns, but only once did he ever hit more than .400. This means that even the great Ted Williams failed more than six times out of every ten he went to bat.

Remember that everything takes time. Even cathedrals are built one brick at a time. Some of our failures can turn out to be successes later on. That argument that you have with your preteenager may later turn out to be a time in which both of you discover important things about each other. The incredible frustration you experience trying to get the kids to do chores around the house can become a great opportunity for teaching (and learning) proper attitudes. The special event you had planned that turned out to be a bomb may be something you can all laugh about a few days from now.

Hang in there, Dad. To paraphrase Teddy Roosevelt:

Stay in the bright sunshine of the arena. Dare the mighty—even "ordinarily mighty"—things. Shun the gray twilight that knows neither victory nor defeat. Go for it and you will know genuine triumph because of one indisputable fact—you have cared enough to be involved with your kids.

Chapter Six Notes

1. Edward R. Dayton, *Tools for Time Management* (Grand Rapids: Zondervan Publishing House, 1974), pp. 80, 68.

What Kids Need Most in a Dad

2. Quote by Theodore Roosevelt as taken from Ted Engstrom's *Pursuit of Excellence* (Grand Rapids: Zondervan Publishing House, 1982), p. 57.

3. David P. Campbell, *If You Don't Know Where You're Going, You'll Probably End Up Somewhere Else* (Allen, Texas: Argus Communications, 1974).

4. Paul Williams, *Das Energi* (New York: Warner Books, Inc., 1978), p. 5.

5. Edward R. Dayton and Ted W. Engstrom, *Strategy for Living* (Ventura, California: Regal Books, 1976), p. 23.

6. For these ideas on purposes versus goals, I am indebted to Edward R. Dayton and Ted W. Engstrom, *Strategy for Living,* chapter 5.

Seven
Tips for the Practical Father
Specifics You Can Do... Starting Now

Until recently, a father's part in raising and nurturing children was given little attention. "Real men" tended to leave the kids to mom—men's job was to work to support the family and when they came home, to mete out the punishment that mom had decreed. Happily for fathers and their children, that attitude is changing. Society now acknowledges that real men do enjoy their kids. There is a growing emphasis on the importance of the bond between fathers and children. They are central to the development of their children who need their love and support. Men are realizing that they, as well as women, need to learn to be parents.

Real Men Enjoy Their Kids[1]

What shall it profit a man if he gain the whole world and lose his own children?

Clyde M. Narramore[2]

If I could change my dad . . . it would be to play with me more often because he hardly plays with me . . . .

Boy, Age Seven[3]

I was teaching a high school psychology course some years ago when one of my students came in amid great frustration and with a pained expression on her face said, "Life is so . . . so . . . so . . . *daily!*"

I have often thought how right she was and still is. Life is very daily for all of us and especially for fathers. *To be a dad means to have problems.* We are to expect them, to lean into them. To be a dad means to have surprises. To be a dad means to be on a risky, zestful adventure, living tiptoe at the edge of expectation for the next round of God's serendipities in your home.

Being a father also means being creative, not letting the daily, ordinary schedule get too routine. In this chapter, as well as chapter 8, I want to throw out a great many ideas, suggestions, plans, and thoughts. The suggestions here are not meant to limit you but to provoke some new thinking on your own that will keep your privilege of fathering from becoming boring—or in some cases overwhelming.

For simplicity's sake, I've decided to give the suggestions alphabetically. We might even call this the "ABCs of Fathering," except that would somehow indicate that fathering is easy and we know that isn't the case. So, here they are—a random but alphabetized stream of ideas and practical tips to help you with your fathering task. Some get very specific and talk about how to make a simple toy, how to play a simple game, and so on. Others are more philosophical and talk about principles and strategy. But I hope they will all be practical and that you will find them helpful in living out the wonderful "dailyness" of your own home.

Oh, yes, one more thing. Paul Lewis of Dad's Only has kindly granted me permission to use or adapt many ideas

SPECIFICS YOU CAN DO . . . STARTING NOW

from the Dad's Only newsletter. Whenever Dad's Only is the source of the idea I'm giving, I put an asterisk after it. I think *very* highly of Paul and his Dad's Only operation. (The Dad's Only newsletter is published monthly. You can subscribe by writing to: Dad's Only, P. O. Box 340, Julian, California 92036. It may be one of the best investments you ever make.)

A **Is for Aerobics**

Use it or lose it, Dad. The key is to pump some new life, new oxygen into your family each day. You might even call it preventive discipline. If your family is fully alive and aware, living out their own adventure, discipline won't be as much of a problem.

For example, when was the last time you took the kids for a hike around the block with the goal of seeing ten things they've never seen before? When was the last time you challenged them to an arm-wrestling match? or kidnapped them for a double-dip ice-cream cone? or challenged them to see who could write the best poem about his or her family?

It's time, Dad, to inhale deeply and breathe some fresh air into your fathering. In aerobics, the concern is always for the heart. Let's hope, when it comes to fathering, that your heart is too big for your body, and that by sheer energy alone, you raise your standards to new levels of boldness and excitement.

A **Is for Attention**

A very wise man was asked, "What's the most important quality in life?" He said simply, "Attention." The questioner didn't understand and so he asked him again, "Well, sir, perhaps I can agree with that, but could you expand it for me?" And the wise man said, "Yes. Attention—attention."

What Kids Need Most in a Dad   111

After a long pause, the inquirer finally asked again, "Sir, could you explain it just a little bit more for me?" To which the wise man said, "Of course: attention—attention—attention."

It's a simple story but ever since I heard it my attention level has gone up. Do you pay attention to your kids? When you're with them are you *all* there?

B Is for Balance

If you want your kids to learn how to live a balanced Christian life as they grow up, try teaching them balance early. It may start out with simple physical exercises like trying to balance a broom on two fingers, or learning how to walk on a two-by-four lying on the ground.

Physical activities can lead into discussions about balance and how we can all stay more balanced in our lives. Some other ideas include having the kids eat dinner one evening, or even a week of evenings, with their nondominant hand. (In other words, if they are right-handed, have them use their left hand.) By using the nondominant hand they learn to use all of their body and to develop both sides of their brain. For fun one evening, have them make place cards for the dinner table with their nondominant hand. Have them include a bit of artwork as well. It will be worth some laughs and make a good conversation piece.

The idea in working on balance is to show your children that there is physical balance and there is also mental, spiritual, and emotional balance. As they grow up, they need all facets of balance in their lives.

B Is for Best

Best refers to those qualities or things that are of the highest degree. *Best* implies excellence, that which is most important.

Probably the best, hence most important, thing you could do right now is to (1) set down this book and (2) go spend some time with your kids. To make the *best* use of that time, plan a specific activity which has something to do with a goal you have for your children.

B Is for Bicycles

Not too long ago I got a bike that I could ride with my kids. For years I've ridden a ten-speed bike for exercise with some of my friends, but the one I bought for riding with my children is a "cruiser" type with balloon tires that I can ride *anywhere.* Police departments frequently have auctions where bikes can be picked up at a very reasonable price. I think it was one of the best investments I've ever made.

Last night I asked my kids, "What are the most fun things we do together?"

"Riding bikes with you" was one of their favorites. It seems so simple, but it's an enjoyable way to be with your children, and it has some nice extra benefits—like getting some exercise!

B Is for Brainstorm

One of the most important steps in problem solving is to brainstorm. When was the last time you sat around with some other fathers you know and brainstormed on the best and worst things you know about fathering?

The rules of brainstorming are simple. Do not judge, and be as creative as possible. List as many ideas as you possibly can. Avoid "shoulds" and "oughts."

You'd be amazed at how many new and fresh ideas you will come up with over dinner or lunch with friends. Make a phone call this week to one or more friends or dads, inviting them to a time of eating and brainstorming together for the purpose of being better fathers.

C Is for Change

Children are living, growing, changing human beings. All too often I forget that. It's hard for me to remember that my children are not only distinctly different from me but also distinctly different from each other, and each of them is going through a particular passage at this point in time in the process of becoming an independent adult.

Dr. Fitzhugh Dodson wrote a fine book called *How to Father*[4] which has been very helpful to me. In it he indicates that our children will go through some very specific stages. Though these steps are not predictable in any scientific sense, they are good indicators to help us understand that the changes in our children's personalities are quite normal.

I highly recommend Dodson's book. I need to remember that my children will have rhythmic periods of dependency —not only on us as parents but also on their peer groups. If I'm to help them navigate their way through these difficult waters, I need to learn as much as I can about each of the stages in their lives and accept them and encourage them as much as possible.

C Is for Compromise

There are two short words to remember with regard to compromise. The first word is *don't*—that is, don't compromise when it comes to being a dad. Don't compromise with the kind of commitments that you have to make to be with your children. And don't compromise on rules and standards. Your children will test you and it's sometimes tempting to let things go because you want to be "a good guy."

The second word to remember with regard to compromise is *do.* As your children approach the teenage years, you have to learn to compromise with their needs, schedules, and opinions. You don't have to give up on your own values, standards, or rules, but you do need to remember that they are growing, becoming individuals in their own right, and they need some flexibility and understanding.

For example, your budding (or full-bloomed) teenager may come up with a conflict in schedule because of something that is going on at school or with a friend. In other cases, your teenager may prefer to do something (a chore, for example) different from the way you would do it. Can you allow your teenager to do it his or her way?

If compromise seems like a paradox, it is, but it is a very real paradox that you must grapple with daily as a dad.

C Is for Creativity

Our kids are going to need massive doses of creativity to cope with the unpredictable future they will be facing. Such things as creative analogies can sharpen verbal skills and bring out thoughts and feelings sometimes difficult to express. Start with everyone stating the relationship between a personal characteristic or a feeling and some other familiar phenomenon.

For example: "I'm as *thin* as a *stick.*" Or, "I'm as *happy* as a *lark.*" Follow it up by passing out slips of paper and ask each family member to complete the following analogies:

Describe yourself using an analogy:

1. Of an object in outer space.
2. Of a kind of food.
3. Of a circus performer.
4. Of a plant.
5. Of an animal.
6. Of a piece of furniture.

In each case, use "I'm as _____ as a _____."*

When it comes to developing writing skills in school or communication skills at home to express deep-seated feelings, little exercises like this will go a long way. (A fine resource for ideas on creativity is the *Creativity Newsletter* by

Anita Halstead, P.O. Box 1952, Lynnwood, Washington 98036.)

D Is for Date Book

Include your family in your date book. Fill your calendar. I know of very few dads who have, in writing, the specific times that they're going to be with their wives and their children. A strong evidence for a dad who is making the best use of his time with his family is that he's got a lot of things written on his calendar that include his family.

For example, next Monday night, while Pam is in school, it says on my calendar, "Plan a miniadventure for Zac and Josh." Saturday night says, "Dinner with Pam." And then in parenthesis I added, "Discuss some creative ideas for this summer."

Another advantage of having it written down in your date book is that it is easier to tell people no. I know so many dads who complain of their time being stolen away by the church and other community responsibilities. The fault is their own. Dot your date book with your priorities—including your family members!

D Is for Decision Making

One of the most important skills your children will ever learn is how to make good decisions. Have a discussion tonight (and frequently) on what it takes to make good decisions and how to be better at it. Ask your children to name three decisions they might be struggling with right now. What is involved? Talk about a pattern for decision making. Basically, there are at least three steps involved in making a decision:

1. Defining the decision to be made.
2. Selecting the best options.
3. Accepting and assessing the consequences.

Help your children analyze their decisions by filtering them through the above process. Support your children in developing the skill of decision making. Whenever possible, give them the responsibility to make their own decisions and take the consequences for them. Even your young children can begin to learn to make good decisions right now.

For example, the younger child can learn how to decide which of two kinds of shoes or boots are most appropriate to wear in wet or cold weather.

In working with your preadolescent child (ages nine to twelve), you can talk about everything from deciding which clothes to wear to what TV programs to watch.

Remember, as your children get older, you want to give them every opportunity to make their *own* decisions. Don't try to dominate them or force them to simply do what you want them to do. Give them a chance to truly make their own choices, even if you know that in some cases the choices will probably turn out unhappily. Let your child live with the decision and thereby learn from experience how to make a better decision next time.

Almost any situation lends itself to the decision-making process. For example, a friend recently told me of a situation in which he had to discipline his child. Although his mind was made up about the need for discipline, he still gave the child a little practice in decision making by saying, "Would you rather walk to your room or have me carry you?"

E Is for Encouragement

Encourage your children at every legitimate opportunity. A friend of mine told me that no permanent positive change can come from negative input. Although our kids definitely need our constructive criticism in large doses, they need even more ample doses of love, affirmation, and encouragement. Asking which is more important, discipline or encouragement, is like asking which wing of an airplane is most important.

Nothing produces success like success, and the power of encouragement is incredible. For example, I attended an evening service at a very large church one Christmas season. I was so excited about the performance that afterward I went up to the man who had been in charge and complimented him enthusiastically on what a fine job he had done. Surprisingly enough, he started to cry. I was so shocked that I began to apologize, but he stopped me and said, "No, son, it's just that you caught me a little bit by surprise for, you see, I've been at this church for *eighteen years* and no one has ever done that before."

Ever since that incident, I have made every possible effort to encourage as many people as I can (especially my children) in specific ways for their growth and accomplishments. At this point, I haven't run into too many people who are suffering from being "overencouraged."

E Is for Expectations

Your expectations should be fairly communicated to your children at all times. One of the great problems in families today is the so-called communication gap. All homes struggle with it, and it is often due to a lack of communicating our expectations to one another.

For example, ask your children if they really understand what your limits, boundaries, hopes—*your expectations*—are. You might be surprised at what they tell you. The longer I teach at conferences, churches, colleges, and seminaries, I become more and more convinced that what is delivered in content and what is received is usually quite different.

For example, when I allow my children to use my tools, I

give them my clear expectations of how and when I want them returned to their proper place. Frequently, when they are in the process of using the tools, I ask them to repeat to me, in *their* words, what my expectations are and what the consequences will be if they fail to meet them.

F Is for File

Start a file or diary of your favorite sayings, quotations, advice on various subjects, articles, stories, cartoons, verses of Scripture, and so on. Use the items that best express the values, priorities, and principles you believe are important to a happy, mature, and fruitful approach to life. Always keep your children in mind as you create your file.

When your child turns thirteen, leaves for college, marries, or on some other special occasion, organize all the material into a scrapbook. Present it to your child as a source of advice and insight that reflects "how dad views life." It will instantly be a treasured possession and will multiply in significance in future years.*

F Is for Fun

Having fun takes creativity. Try different approaches. I read somewhere that a study showed that people who took different routes to work each day stayed more creative than those who kept going the same way. Don't ever forget the importance of surprise and creativity. Break the routine often. Be willing to be spontaneous and you will definitely have some fun.

Here are some examples:

1. Have everyone in the family eat dinner tonight with their nondominant hands (that is, if they're right-handers, have them eat with their left hands).

2. Surprise your family by "kidnapping" them for breakfast some morning next week.

3. Have a special "Celebrate Tuesday" party with all the trimmings, for no reason other than just reminding your family how much you enjoy being the dad.

4. Bring pencils and paper to dinner some night and have everybody draw his or her version of what the family looks like. Then have them make paper airplanes out of their drawings and have a contest to see whose airplane can fly the farthest.

There are as many ways to have fun as there are grains of sand on the seashore. Take every opportunity to put fun into your family.

G Is for Gifts

Gifts are something given to us, but we can't always hold them in our hands. The most important gifts that we ever received are the unique talents and abilities God gave us. Are you helping your children discover and understand their unique gifts and talents and how they can best use them?

I've heard Dr. James Dobson say that one of the best ways for children to understand what their gifts are is to give them a lot of experiences when they're young so they can see where their interests and abilities really lie. Your children may never know whether or not they have musical gifts, if you don't give them an opportunity to experience music firsthand. They may never know about certain physical, mental, or social skills unless they're given opportunities to explore them.

For example, our son Zac did not realize that he has a

real gift in swimming until we enrolled him in a community class. This fall we're hoping to enroll both boys in music classes so they can explore their possible talents in that area.

Give your children as many experiences as possible. When they find a gift or talent that is really theirs, let them explore it as fully as they can. Don't assume that school is the only place that can bring out the gifts or talents of your children. Their abilities in art, mechanics, and other areas may not come out at school, but they just might blossom under your own encouragement and training.

G **Is for Gratitude**

If I were limited to only one letter in this Alphabet of Fathering I would take the G for gratitude. I know of no other single practice that can bring more joy and peace than gratitude. Gratitude is a discipline; it's an art. Like anything else good in life, it takes work, effort, and practice.

When writing to the Philippians Paul said:

> *Delight yourselves in the Lord, yes, find your joy in him at all times. . . . Don't worry over anything whatever; whenever you pray tell God every detail of your needs in thankful prayer, and the peace of God, which surpasses human understanding, will keep constant guard over your hearts and minds as they rest in Christ Jesus.*
>
> *Philippians 4:4, 6, 7 PHILLIPS*

Paul is clearly saying here that peace is the result of being thankful and full of gratitude. Another way of thinking about it is that thankfulness is the source of the peace we all seek. Thankfulness is the conduit through which the gift of peace can pervade our lives.

I know of no other way to bring joy to my family than through the development of a deep sense of appreciation and thankfulness for each member of the family. We are told that God is enthroned on the praises of Israel.[5] Enthrone Him on the praises of your family by teaching them in word and deed Paul's advice: "Be joyful always; pray continually; give thanks in all circumstances, for this is God's will for you in Christ Jesus" (1 Thessalonians 5:16–18 NIV).

In fact, I think we can go so far as to say that gratitude is not simply an option for a Christian. For those of us fathers who want to be the best we can be, gratitude is one of the most practical and important arts that we can develop.

So, start today in the small areas and in the little ways. When was the last time, for example, that you thanked God for the health of your children? for the many little things your wife does to keep your family on a daily schedule? for your job? for any number of things that we tend to take for granted and seldom think about?

Open your eyes and heart—open them wide. Ask God to teach you how to be more grateful. Begin to look for countless opportunities to thank Him for all the little daily miracles that are part of being alive. It may be subtle at first, but I can virtually *guarantee* you that it will begin to have an effect on your family that is difficult to measure.

H Is for Helpers

If there is anything a Christian family should develop together it is the art of helping one another. Let your kids know that they are not only loved but they are needed as well. Without their efforts, the family strength will be impaired and hampered. Help them realize it's their job as well as yours to make the family go.

Kids need responsibilities to help that are matched to their ages. Even a preschooler can learn how to help pick up toys and empty the garbage. As children get older, their helping responsibilities can grow. Whenever possible, make chores fun. Affirm your children often and hold them to their responsibilities. Help them have a high view of helping—of being part of making the family go. If possible, make a little chart and create a system for giving stars or some sort of recognition for a job well done. (Avoid money and material reward.)

Whenever possible, divide and rotate the least desirable as well as the most popular tasks equally among all family members. If you are just starting a chore system, involve everyone in the planning. List various tasks and problems and talk about why everyone needs to share the load. Remember that children carry out duties they have set for themselves much more readily than those that are imposed upon them. You can even help your children decide what the penalties will be for chores neglected or poorly done.*

H Is for Hink-Pink

Another way to develop the creativity our kids will need in the future is through games. Word games such as Hink-Pink are a lot of fun to play around the dinner table or while making the miles zip by a little faster in the car.

You play Hink-Pink by joining two words of one syllable that rhyme (the Hink-Pink) and then have a brief definition or synonym for each word (the clues). One person gives only the clues while others guess what Hink-Pink he has in mind. Examples:

"I have a Hink-Pink for an unhappy-hippie home." (Answer: sad-pad.)

"I have a Hink-Pink for a happy-parent." (Answer: glad-dad.)

As your children master the one-syllable words, you can

move on to bigger game. Two-syllable words are Hinky-Pinkies. Example: "I have a Hinky-Pinky for a bee's product and currency." (Answer: honey-money.)

If you want to try three-syllable words, call them Hinkaty-Pinkaties. Example: "A Hinkaty-Pinkaty for a citrus drink and a tart jam." (Answer: lemonade-marmalade.)

When you are really ambitious, try four-syllable words which are Hinkadilly-Pinkadillies. Example: "A Hinkadilly-Pinkadilly for a lexicon and a word describing a handed-down story." (Answer: dictionary-legendary.)

Should Hink-Pink wear you down while driving, a simple game to play is a version of "Alphabet." Start with one child who has to find the letter A on anything *outside* of the car —on signs, stores, bumper stickers, and so on. The next person has to find the letter B—*outside* the car. Go through the entire alphabet and the entire family. Remember, everyone must find his or her letter before the next person can play. After completing the alphabet, do it again only make it more challenging. This time through, each letter has to be at the *beginning* of a word that the player finds outside the car. (You may want to allow players to use license plates, particularly for letters like X and Q when time becomes a factor.)

I Is for Inventory

Taking inventory is something we do when we want to know where we stand, how far we've come, and what we have. Do you know where you stand with your children at this point in their lives? in yours? For example:

1. Measure your degree of closeness with each of your children on a scale of 1 to 10. What specific things could you do to increase this closeness—if you feel you need to?

2. What personal and professional interests do you have that might be integrated into your child's growth and development? Have your children ever visited your place of work? Can they explain to their friends what you do for a living?

3. What is the favorite activity you do with each of your children? What do they like to do best with you? Have you ever asked them, "What's the most fun thing you do with me?"

4. What is your favorite time of day with your children and why?

5. How much time did you spend with each of your children last week?

It doesn't hurt to take inventory like this every two or three months. It may help you change your routine or add something that is needed.

J Is for Joshua

Joshua means "the Lord is my salvation." It is the Old Testament version of the name for Jesus. Joshua is a strong and marvelous name. It is the handle we gave to our younger son when he was born six years ago.

Our Joshua is athletic and always on the go. Right now he's learning to read with an intensity that I almost envy. He loves life with abandonment. At the age of four he learned how to ride a bike and before we knew it he was doing "wheelies" off our deck. At the age of five he was jumping off the high-dive board. He loves to wrestle and he is sometimes so involved with living out his life that he forgets to eat. Josh is one of the two very specific reasons I enjoy the privilege of being a father (*see* Zachary, page 161).

What Kids Need Most in a Dad   125

Josh loves his brother, although he drives him nuts half the time. Josh loves his mother, although he drives her nuts most of the time. I'll never forget the time Josh saw a picture of me, Zac, and Pam, who was very pregnant at the time. With great concern, Josh asked, "Where was I?"

Zac said, "Well, you were in her tummy, silly," as he pointed to Pam's pregnant stomach.

Josh, who was only four at the time, asked with the wonderful honesty of childhood, "What was I doing in there?"

Zac said, as only an older brother could, "Well, you were getting borned, Josh."

Immediately Josh threw his shoulders back and said, "Oh, yeah," as if he understood everything. Then, smiling with a twinkle in his eye, he looked over at Zac and said, "And you know what I was saying, Zac? *Hey! Let me out of here!*"

That's the kind of kid our Josh is. We're so lucky God decided to have him come live with us, because we know that with him life will always be an adventure.

J Is for Journal

Keep a journal or notebook on your family. It's a great place to keep track of some of the wonderful anecdotes that happen in every family. But perhaps the best use of a journal is to help your child develop self-esteem. Record some purposes and goals that you have for your children. Break down those larger purposes into specific goals and activities that you can accomplish within certain time frames.

For example, you may want to get them into a music or athletic program so they can develop skills that will contribute to their self-esteem. Maybe you want them to meet certain individuals who model self-confidence and self-esteem in an excellent way. Perhaps you want them to read certain books of the Bible, or other good books, and then report back to you on what they read. Every once in a while show them how much progress they have made, and how proud you are to be their dad.

Whatever goals you set for your children, remember that you are trying to help them build self-esteem—you are not trying to build your own pride and ego. If you push them too hard on meeting goals that you may have set for them, it will only tear down their esteem and make them feel less confident.

Map out your hopes for your children and develop a flexible and nonjudgmental approach. Be willing to change your plans as you go along, according to your children's abilities, limitations, and so on. And keep it all recorded in your journal. It will make practical as well as memorable reading further down the line.

J **Is for Joy**

I don't want my kids to grow up "wanting to be happy." If that sounds a bit startling, I'm glad because I meant to get your attention. The root of the word *happy* comes from the same root as the word *happening.* In other words, happiness depends on external events and circumstances that happen to us. We are at the mercy of these events.

I want my children to grow up seeking joy. Jesus promises in John 15:11, "I have told you this so that my joy may be in you and that your joy may be complete" (NIV). The joy taught in the New Testament is distinctly different from happiness. *Joy occurs in spite of circumstances, not because of circumstances or happenings.*

I want my kids to learn the quality of joy. I want them to grow up to be men of great joy and to be able to say with Nehemiah, "The joy of the Lord is my strength" (*see* Nehemiah 8:10). Note that Nehemiah did not say, "Happiness is my strength." Happiness is an external, circumstantial kind of thing that can fade in the first rain. But joy is a deep kind of quality that we choose and partake of in spite of circumstances and events.

Even at their young ages, I am trying to help my sons understand the difference between the happiness they experience when they get a new toy and the joy they experience from a genuine achievement or understanding how something works. I want them to know the difference between the happiness that occurs when a friend likes them and the joy they can experience when they learn how to really like a friend.

All of this may sound a bit subtle and as if there is a fine line between the two qualities of joy and happiness. The line may be hard to find, but it is not a fine one. Joy will last, happiness will fade. I want my boys to understand that— starting now.

K Is for Kid Acceptance

What do kids need most from a dad? At the bottom line, more than anything else, they want and need acceptance. Genuine kid acceptance requires your unconditional love. You can find the term *unconditional love* in a lot of books these days. You don't find as much of it as you should in family circles. Let's be honest; it is hard to love anyone "unconditionally." We have expectations. We have standards. We are human. We do set conditions.

But that doesn't mean we can't work harder at kid acceptance. I think working hard at accepting my kids is a very special art. As a graffiti item I saw on a wall the other day put it, "Life ain't no exact science." Life is always changing, always moving, never static. There will always be problems to cope with and my children will always be making mistakes of one kind or another. Come to think of it, so will I.

128   What Kids Need Most in a Dad

No matter what the age of my kids, I need to accept them for who they are in spite of the warts, the blemishes, the mistakes, the "bad scenes."

Even though unconditional love may be an ideal that is far above my reach, I reach anyway. I reach because kids of all ages will go wherever they can find acceptance. You see, acceptance is like a magnet. Why do teenagers end up with the wrong crowd? Because the crowd accepts them for who they are. Let your kids know they are unique and accept them as they are. How? For openers, the next time your son or daughter really blows it, let the first thing you say be, "Hey, I love you." You don't have to congratulate him or her for blowing it, but on the other hand, you don't have to dwell on criticizing and correcting beyond what is necessary. He probably feels bad enough already. Do everything you can to let your child know that his performance is one thing, but your love never changes.

K **Is for Know Your Kids**

How much do you really know about your child? Take your son or daughter out to breakfast or even dinner this week and discover the following (if you don't know already):

1. What makes your child really angry?
2. Who is your child's hero or heroes? Why?
3. What is your child's biggest fear?
4. By what names is your child called at school or among his peers?
5. What is your child's favorite book?
6. What person outside of your family influences your child the most?
7. How and where would your child most like to

spend a day? (If possible, plan to do just that soon.)

8. What embarrasses your child and why?
9. What would your child like most from you?
10. What is your child's most prized possession?

Taking a look at these ten basic questions will give you some insight as to how well you really know your child.*

L Is for Long-Distance

Many dads—due to job pressures or family problems and breakups—have to learn how to love their kids long-distance. The finest thing I've ever found for practical help with this problem is a little book by George Newman called *One Hundred and One Ways to Be a Long-Distance Super-Dad.*[6] Newman gives 101 practical tips on maintaining a close relationship with your children even though you are separated by time and/or distance. He suggests everything from armchair baseball to chess via the mail to a game of twenty questions with miniletters.

If you're one of those dads who has to be gone a lot (as I do on occasion), get a copy of this book and put some of the ideas into practice. Your phone and postage bills may go up, but it will be more than worth it.

L Is for Love

Love is quite likely the most used word in books on parenting and families. But here is a question I have always found interesting: "Do you know how your wife and your children *perceive* love?"

Very often, there is a distinct difference between the way someone gives love and the way the other person perceives love. For example, I tend to be on the romantic side and enjoy doing things with high emotional content. My wife, on the other hand, is likely to perceive love that is clothed more in practical realities. For example, to Pam it is a much more loving thing for me to be on time than to be late and bring a dozen roses.

I asked my boys recently how they perceived love. Zac said, "It's when you tell me so." Josh said, "It's when you do things with me." I am willing to bet that most children would answer about the same as Zac and Josh did—particularly along the lines of "doing things with me." It's when we do things *with* our children that they perceive we love them. We can say we love them—and it is oh, so important to do so—but if we don't follow through by actually being there, by spending time, by showing interest, by listening, the word *love* will start to have a hollow ring.

Take some time today and ask your wife how *she* perceives love the best. And also take time to ask your kids how *they* know you love them and what is the best way for you to show it. I guarantee the time will be well spent.

That takes care of the first twelve letters of the alphabet. We'll do the last fourteen in chapter 8.

Chapter Seven Notes

1. Wenda Goodhart Singer, Stephen Shechtman, Mark Singer, *Real Men Enjoy Their Kids* (Nashville: Abingdon Press, 1983), p. 16.

2. Clyde M. Narramore, quoted in Dad's Only newsletter, Volume I, Number 7 (July 1978), p. 1.

3. Erwin Lutzer, *If I Could Change My Mom and Dad* (Chappaqua, New York: Christian Herald, 1982), p. 45.

4. Fitzhugh Dodson, *How to Father* (New York: New American Library, 1975).

5. Psalms 22:3, *New International Version,* particularly the footnote on this verse.

6. George Newman, *One Hundred and One Ways to Be a Long-Distance Super-Dad* (Mountain View, California: Blossom Valley Press, 1981).

Eight

More Tips for the Practical Father

Including the Mother's Role in Fathering

If I don't take time to step back
And evaluate my everyday
The shape of my life
I lose what's important
in the daily routine.

I forget what I need to remember
And the things I really want
My child to know
To care about
Go unsaid
Unseen
Unknown.

Cindy Herbert and Susan Russell[1]

We are all functioning at a small fraction of our capacity to live fully in its total meaning of loving, caring, creating and adventuring. Consequently, the actualizing of our potential can become the most exciting adventure of our lifetime.

Herbert Otto[2]

I would like [my parents] to see there is a difference between being good parents and being overly strict parents. They think that if they are nice to you they aren't being good. Most parents listen to their kids and try to understand. Mine don't.

Girl, Age Twelve[3]

One of the frustrating things about doing an Alphabet of Fathering is that the possibilities for practical ideas, suggestions, and tips are virtually endless. We covered twelve letters of the alphabet in chapter 7, and now we'll go on to the last fourteen, but as we do so I'm painfully aware that there are so many other tips I could give if I had space.

As I go along, I try to include some of my own personal favorites and, as you can tell, I ride a few personal hobbyhorses. I can only hope I'm not leaving out anything or anyone important. To be sure, we don't want to leave out one of the most important tips of all, and that's why this chapter starts with some comments on a very important person in every child's life.

M Is for Mom

They've been called "mothers," "mom," "ma," and by other various handles. It is quite obvious that none of us would ever be parents without them. Mothers not only play the crucial part in the birth of our children but also in their development.

At several points in previous chapters I've talked about the need for us dads to join our wives in being a substantial part of our children's lives. I believe the key to the parenting process is to work closely with your wife to establish a complementary balance of responsibilities. Dad cannot turn over most or all of the responsibility to Mom (although too many dads do just that). On the other hand, if Dad does get turned on and wants to get involved, how does he do it without usurping Mom's responsibilities or undermining her gifts and talents? If your kids are blessed to have two parents in the home—which many do not, these days—it is important that the two of you work together creatively to maximize the parenting effect. Here are some suggestions for how to do just that.

1. *When was the last time you and your wife sat down and talked about your goals as parents?* Are you mutually committed to strong specific goals and objectives? Have you ever discussed the difference in your styles of parenting and how you can complement each other rather than be in conflict? Who is responsible for discipline in the home? How is the discipline accomplished? Are you backing each other up when discipline is necessary? Children have an uncanny ability to detect lack of agreement between their parents and they will do everything they can to play you against each other. Make a solemn vow together that you will always back each other up, even if one doesn't particularly think the other is completely right in a certain situation. Later, if you want to discuss your differences, do it privately, out of earshot of the children.

2. *If you could change three things about your wife, what would they be?* If she could change three things about you, what would they be? Have the two of you ever sat and talked about questions like these? Why not try it soon and zero in on the area of the children, if possible? What would you like to change about each other in regard to parenting style, philosophy, procedure, and so on?

3. *What are you doing to support your wife's role as a mother?* What is she doing to support and encourage your

role as a father? For example, what are you doing to encourage your wife's personal development and growth? Do you sometimes take over responsibilities in the home so that she can be free to have time for herself, possibly time to take a class or get some exercise? These are *not* small areas. The stereotype of the housebound housewife slowly going bonkers with her preschoolers is all too true. Don't let it happen in your home.

4. *What are some of the gray areas that exist in your parenting responsibilities?* As mentioned above, our kids have an amazing ability to discover these gray areas and to exploit them. If Mom and Dad aren't clear on certain procedures and standards, there will be continual tension and hassles. How can you and your wife better define and clarify some of these gray areas and figure out which parent is better suited for a particular task? Sit down with your wife and talk about your individual strengths and weaknesses. If she were to write a list of fifteen things that bug her most about you, would there be any surprises? What about your list of fifteen things? How does your wife support or resist your role as a father? Talk about these questions openly and it will make a strong difference, not only in how you rear the children but in your marriage as well.

5. *How aware are you of your wife's feelings?* Charlie and Martha Shedd spend fifteen minutes each day just talking about feelings and staying in touch with each other's emotions. Practice the art of asking each other good questions. (For an excellent list of open-ended questions, *see* "Q Is for Questions," page 143.) Do you know, for example, some of your wife's biggests dreams? What are some of her biggest frustrations? What are her biggest hopes for the children? And what are some of her biggest disappointments and problems in rearing the children? Then share your dreams, frustrations, hopes, and disappointments.

What Kids Need Most in a Dad

What does your wife worry about? What do you worry about? Spend time talking these questions through.

6. *Spend some particular time on your individual strengths and weaknesses as parents.* In the business world, companies always try to place a person where his or her strengths are maximized and weaknesses diminished. You can use the same strategy in your family. For example, if one of you is on the more permissive side, the more authoritative parent should do more of the disciplining and confronting of the children when they are out of line. If Mom is the weaker disciplinarian and is with the kids most of the day, this can be a problem. Dad will have to back her up and encourage her to move in and discipline on the spot, while the infraction is still fresh in the child's mind. The last thing Dad should do, however, is come home expecting his wife to have "taken care of all that" throughout the day. If she has to share a discipline problem, listen carefully, back her up, and do additional disciplining yourself if it is necessary. Again, the idea is to work together and complement each other instead of feeling put out or inconvenienced.

7. *Finally, talk together about specific things you can do to assist your wife in her role as a mother.* Then talk about specific things she can do to assist you in your role as a dad. Work on these things and then check back later to see how you are doing.

8. *It's been said often but it bears repeating: "The best thing a dad can do for his kids is to love their mother."* When was the last time you brought her flowers—just to say "I love you" or "Thanks for being such a great wife and mother"? Do you have a regular night each week for just the two of you to sneak away?

In the Alphabet of Fathering, M is always primarily for Mom. We men can't become fathers without a mom and we can't do our job without them, either.

N Is for Never

We've been told all too often to never say never. I disagree. I would like to encourage you to say never in certain situations, and often. For example, *never give up.* Nothing beats perspiration and perseverance in fathering. I would also like to say *never give in.* In other words, strive to continue to be the unique dad that God made you to be. Don't give in to compromise or comparison. Never give in to those myths and illusions that would have you believing you are called to be someone else. Never give in to the people who want to put you in certain boxes or slots, no matter how good their reasons may sound.

Then I'd like to say it is *never too soon to start.* Procrastination is one of the great diseases of our age. If you've gotten this far in this book, you should have a lot of ideas and desires to be a better dad. Start now—it's never too soon.

Finally, I'd like to say it is *never too late.* It is never too late to start doing what is right. I don't care how many failures you and I have had as dads. I don't care how dismal the circumstances have been. I don't care how difficult it is right now. It is never, never, never, never too late to start doing it over again. Life has a phenomenal capacity to regenerate itself. Miracles can still happen. We live on *this side of Easter,* which means anything can happen. So, the next time someone tells you never to say never, tell them to never do it again.

N Is for Nipping Things in the Bud

Gardeners have taught us for a long time that it's easier if we nip things in the bud. It may be a simple thing to pull up a little seedling with only a few roots, but if we wait until it's a gigantic bush or tree, we may be in for a struggle.

Develop the art of responding to disciplinary situations

What Kids Need Most in a Dad

when they happen. This obviously requires presence and a little courage. But I think the more children see our consistency of discipline and insistence on continuity, the more they appreciate it.

A key to consistency is having rules for your home that are clearly understood by your children. Roy Lessin writes:

> *House rules are like a pole that is placed alongside a long plant growing in the garden. The pole is not there to stop the plant's development, but to help guide it into maturity and productivity. House rules provide an important base from which to develop obedience. They let a child know where he stands and help to create both a sense of freedom and security. A child does not really care which house rules are made, but he does need to know what they are.*[4]

It is best if there are few (probably less than six) very clear rules which are mutually understood by everyone in the family. Tim Timmons says he has two sets of rules which are very clear to his kids. One, no lying—ever. The truth is always to be spoken no matter what the consequences are. Two, each person is to learn to accept the responsibility and the consequences for his or her own behavior.

House rules may include such things as always picking up after yourself, or always eating meals when they're served, or always letting others know where you are going. Sit down with your wife and your kids and develop a list of mutually agreed upon house rules. Then hold one another accountable to them. You'll be surprised at the clarity and freedom it gives to your family.

N Is for No

No is one of the greatest words in the English language, especially for dads. *No* is very simple and to the point. The problem is that it needs to be applied in the right time and the right place. In the past few decades, *no* hasn't been applied enough, and we're paying the price.

When I was growing up (in a very affirmative environment, by the way) *no* was a word that my brother and I knew was final. I can't remember a single instance when my parents changed their minds, once they had said no.

I'll never forget the time, in my early teens, when I presented a wild-eyed fanciful scheme to my folks. My friend Bill French and I were going to ride our bikes across Seattle and then take the ferry across Puget Sound. Then we planned to ride thirteen miles to Panther Lake, where he and I would spend the weekend camping by ourselves. I was thirteen at the time and it all seemed like quite an adventure to me. My folks listened attentively and when I was finished, simply said, "No." I began to walk away when Bill said to me, "Tim, you didn't even try. Come on, let's go back and explain it again. If we only badger them a little bit more, I'm sure they'll let us do it."

I said to Bill, with as much security and pride as anything else, that he didn't understand. We could have stood there talking from then until doomsday and the answer would always be the same.

That knowledge gave me great security as I grew up. I can't explain it any further, except to say that I hope I pass on that same sort of strength, firmness, and security to my kids.

O Is for Olympics

If you need a family fun night idea, how about developing a backyard or living room Olympics? All it takes is a little bit of creativity, a roll of masking tape, a wristwatch that measures seconds, a yardstick or tape measure, and a few extra things like paper plates, sheets of paper, and felt-tip markers. If you want, prepare make-believe gold, silver, and bronze medals to hang around the necks of the winners. It all depends on how fancy you want to be.

Your home-style Olympics can include such events as a standing one-foot broad jump, a standing two-foot broad jump, or a discus throw with a paper plate. If you're in the backyard, use a large rock for a shot put. If you're in your living room, use a wad of paper. Set up obstacle courses and see who can cover them in the best time.*

The possibilities for Olympic events of this kind are almost limitless. For a more complete version of how to create your home Olympics, write to the Dad's Only newsletter and ask for the December 1979 issue.[5]

P Is for Patient Endurance

I remember some years ago on a New Year's Eve, several of us were discussing what we thought are the greatest of all Christian attributes. Many of the standard ones, like faith, hope, and love, came up. My wife was the last to speak and she surprised me by saying, "Patient endurance." Since then, however, I've come to believe that patient endurance is definitely an important virtue for any Christian and practically indispensable for a Christian parent. Parenting is possibly the finest crucible we'll ever have for learning the quality of patient endurance. Every day parents face disappointment and the realities of having things fail to work out quite as expected.

For an excellent statement on patient endurance, try the words of Paul. When writing to the Roman Christians, Paul said that knowing God in Christ didn't just give us hope for the future. ". . . we can be full of joy here and now even in our trials and troubles. These very things will give us patient endurance; this in turn will develop a mature character, and a character of this sort produces a steady hope, a hope that will never disappoint us" (Romans 5:3–5 PHILLIPS).

To be a dad means you will be disappointed. But the very measure of your character will be your ability to accept the disappointments with patient endurance. Face the inevitable trials and troubles in *the right spirit* and you will develop steady hope and maturity in Christ.

I not only want to model these thoughts from Romans 5 for my children but I want them to develop the same qualities as well. The next time your child faces a real disappointment, why not pull out this section of the book and read it together? Better yet, why not pull out the Book itself and read Romans 5:1–6 together? Then discuss the process of developing the kind of maturity, character, and patient endurance that won't fade under pressure.

P **Is for Plan**

I have a little acronym that I often use when I think about my family. It utilizes the letters P L A N.

P means prepare with a passion. I often think about this as I drive home from work. I can't wait to be with my kids. I want to be mentally prepared and have plenty of enthusiasm when I see them.

L means to live each moment to the fullest (for I know that that moment will never be ours again).

A means to act as if each moment will influence the rest of your child's life—because it will.

N means that now is the time to begin. Now is the only time I have—so I want to jump in and use it to the fullest.

I've used my P L A N acronym often, especially when I haven't had a lot of time for lengthy planning with pencil and paper. Often I'll think of these four simple letters while in the car on the way home. As I do this, it helps me slow down, unwind, and refocus. It usually helps me come up with one or two simple things I can do with my family that evening—and that is usually enough.

P Is for Plant a Tree

Plant a tree in honor of his or her next birthday. It will not only give your son or daughter something to care for but it will also provide a long-lasting reminder of a very special day. It will give you some interesting perspectives on life as the tree and your child grow up.

P Is for Place to Talk

A place to talk can be a beautiful tool for keeping channels of communication open between you and your children. Start to notice the places where your children seem most willing to share their thoughts with you. Then try to go to these places with your children more often. Pretty soon you both may start acknowledging those places as "our talking spot." It may be a chair in the family room, or perhaps the bed in the bedroom. It can be a bench in the backyard, or a certain route you take on a walk. Wherever it is, it will always be a special place to build your relationship.*

Some families have also developed a "reconciliation rug," which means that when there is an argument between two family members, they can join each other on the rug and try to reconcile their differences.

Q Is for Questions

An art that has become almost extinct in our educational system, whether in school or in the family, is that of asking *good* questions. We have become an answer-oriented society, passively sitting in front of the television set or in front

CHAPTER EIGHT

of experts, waiting for someone to give us "the answer." Many times, however, we have forgotten the question!

The art of asking good questions is something I highly recommend to dads who would like to be more creative and effective. I think questions are one of the best ways to get involved with your children, understand who they are, and help them discover some goals and directions for life.

First, let's look at a few basics on the difference between good questions and not-so-good questions. Good questions are open-ended. Good questions give the other person a number of possibilities and ways in which to respond. Not-so-good questions are closed. For example, when you ask, "How are you?" the answer is usually a simple, "Fine." A better way to ask that same question is, "If you could describe your life today according to a weather pattern or forecast, how would it sound?"

In short, good questions invite the more creative response. Poor questions invite the trite, hackneyed, or very brief response. A poor question can often be answered with a yes or no, and the person answering does little to share or reveal himself. A good question tends to help the other person dip into his well of values, attitudes, and feelings.

At Summit Expedition, the instructors spend a great deal of time practicing the art of asking good questions. During our wilderness courses, our instructors utilize the skills of dialogue rather than just holding forth with monologues. The success or failure of a course often depends on how creative and gifted the instructor is at the art of asking good questions and getting meaningful dialogue going.

The following list of questions is based on the kinds of questions we try to ask during our Summit Expedition courses. Some of them may be a bit too advanced for the ages of your children, but I'm sure you could adapt many of these questions and still use them during your family times.

What Kids Need Most in a Dad

1. If you could take a trip, where would you go and why? (With younger children, make the trip across town or maybe to another state. With older children, suggest a trip across the country or around the world.)
2. How do you usually feel about yourself when you wake up? How do you feel about life— going to school, living at home, and so on?
3. If you could change three things about yourself (how you look, how you act, and so forth) what would you change and why?
4. In what ways will you be different ten years from now?
5. What are your strengths? What are your weaknesses?
6. What is the nicest compliment you ever received?
7. When did God become real to you and how did it happen? Or, how do you think God can become more real and personal to you?
8. What does the word *love* mean to you?
9. What does the word *peace* mean to you?
10. What does the word *freedom* mean to you?
11. What is one of the biggest disappointments you've ever faced and how did you handle it?
12. What is one of your biggest dreams? What are some of your ultimate goals in life?
13. When other people look at you, what do they think? How do you think other people describe you?
14. If you had to sum up your life or describe your life in five words, what would they be?
15. What are three things that make you smile?
16. Who are some of your heroes? What people have influenced your life the most?

What Kids Need Most in a Dad

17. What are some of the most important decisions that have influenced your life?
18. What are three things that frustrate you the most?
19. What embarrasses you? Can you think of one of your most embarrassing moments?
20. What do you like most (or least) about school?
21. If you could do five things to change the world, what would they be?
22. When you want to cheer yourself up, what do you do?
23. Have you ever wanted something you couldn't have? How did you respond?
24. If you could describe yourself as a color, what color would you be?
25. If you could describe yourself as a car, what kind of a car would you be?
26. What comic strip character best describes you? (And the possibilities for these are endless: What kind of movie, TV show, game, commercial, and so on.)
27. If there were a fire in the home, what five things would you make sure you took with you?
28. What are five of the things that bug you most about adults?
29. What are five of the things that bug you most about people your age?
30. If you could change your name, would you? What would you change it to?
31. What are two things you want from God? What are two things you think God wants from you?
32. If you could draw a picture of God, what do you think He'd look like?

What Kids Need Most in a Dad

33. Have you ever really been mad at God?
    Have you ever really felt loved by God?
34. When Christ looks at you, what does He
    think? If He wanted to whisper something in
    your ear, what would He say?
35. If you could change three things about your
    parents, what would they be?
36. If you could do three things to change
    your life right now, what would they be
    and why?
37. What's the best movie you've ever seen and
    why? What's the best book you've ever read
    and why?
38. If you could change five things about your
    school or church, what would they be?
39. What are four things you like most about your
    parents? What are four things you would like
    to see them change?
40. What do your parents do to enhance your
    life and what do they do to inhibit your life?
41. What are six things you're glad you *don't*
    have?
42. What are ten things you're really thankful for?

As you see, the possibilities are endless. Always try and leave the question open-ended, but make it *specific* enough to obtain a response. For example, it is better to ask about a number of things such as, "If you could sum up your life in *five* words . . ." rather than simply say, "Describe your life." The numbers that you use in your questions are obviously arbitrary. But a question like, "Tell me about *three* of your fears," is a better question than simply making the question totally open-ended, such as, "Tell me what you're afraid of."

Like any art, asking questions takes practice. Practice

being interested in your kids and demonstrate your interest by asking creative questions. Keep your questions current. Practice them at mealtimes. One of the games we sometimes play at our house at mealtimes is Twenty Questions. Family members get to ask one person in the family twenty questions that they have to answer. This is a great way to not only practice asking questions but to also get the whole family involved with one another. And what you find out is often enlightening!

R **Is for Relational Goals**

The goals you set for your family don't always have to be utilitarian. That is, you don't always have to have a definite time, a definite program or project. Sometimes your goal may simply be to just play with your kids, just laugh with them, just be with them.

In other words, don't be afraid of "doing nothing." In many cases, as you "do nothing" with your children, you are doing the most important thing of all—building your relationship with them. Relational goals are just as important, if not more important, than specific projects or task-oriented goals.

For example, one of my goals is to tuck my kids into bed every night that I am home. One of the most important times (and often the most overlooked) is that time just before going to sleep. This is a wonderful time for Dad to spend ten or fifteen minutes just talking and listening to his children. You may not accomplish much, but don't worry about that. Our task- and goal-oriented society drives us all day long to get something done and be somewhere on time. But take a few moments with your children to just relate, talk, play, and maybe even laugh and roughhouse a little. The influence of these relational times is practically inestimable.

R Is for Reminiscing

Instead of TV tonight, invest in an hour after dinner reminiscing about when each family member: (1) had the most fun; (2) felt the most embarrassed; (3) cried the hardest; (4) was so tired that _____; (5) never worked harder; and (6) felt the closest to God.

The family scrapbook or photo albums can embellish the sharing or jog your memory. Close by thanking God for the love, privileges, and protection He has given each family member.*

R Is for Round Table

Children not only need discipline but they need to understand it—in their own terms. When I was younger my folks instituted "Round Table" discussions for those times when Steve and I misbehaved (and if other children were involved they were included as well). The rules were simple:

1. Each of us had to express *in our own words* what we had done wrong, and possibly why.
2. Each of us had input as to what *we* thought our punishment should be.

Then together, a decision was reached which was both fair and well understood—elements which may be helpful in your family as well.

S Is for Sex Education

The sum total of my sex education at home occurred one night when my parents came into the living room to talk to my brother and me. Stumbling for words, my mother finally said, "Well, Dad wants to talk to you about the birdies and the bees." When my dad didn't know what to say, Mom finally turned away in frustration and said, "Oh, well, they probably know more about it than we do."

That, in truth, is the sum total of the sex education I can remember getting at home. Is the sex education of your preadolescent on schedule? Notice I said *preadolescent.* If you wait until they hit the teenage years, it may be too late. They already probably do know more than you do— or at least more of the wrong kind of information than you want them to know. Here are some things that you and your wife should agree upon concerning sex education:

1. *What terminology is to be used at what age level for certain body parts and functions?*

2. *At what ages should our children understand the meaning of words like breasts, penis, ovaries, uterus, climax, semen, and so on?* When describing body parts in particular, it's always good to start using the correct words when your children are very young.

3. *At what age will you discuss in detail with each child the sex act?* Don't fool yourself by saying, "Well, there's plenty of time for that." The time will go by with incredible speed and before you know it, your best opportunities will be gone.

4. *What will be taught about personal chastity, necking, impure thoughts, marriage, masturbation, contraception, abortion, French kissing, homosexuality, pornography, X-rated movies—and when?* It is very important for you and your wife to sit down and not only talk about this in detail but also put together a schedule that you can use in talking to your kids about their sex education.*

You might be saying at this point, "Yes, all that sounds good, but just how do I go about it?" There are many excellent books on the market which cover sex education. One of the best of the newer ones is *How to Teach Your Child About Sex* by Grace H. Ketterman, M.D. (Fleming H. Revell Company, 1981).

S Is for Sensorama

We have five senses, but it seems we rarely use four of them. Statistics show that we get about 90 percent of our input through our eyes, and even then we don't see as well as we could. Take your kids for a walk around the block, or for several blocks, and emphasize each of the different senses. For example, walk around one block *smelling* as many new things as you can. If you have more than one child, you can create a little friendly competition by saying, "See who can smell the most smells."

Then walk around another block trying to *hear* as many things as you can. Keep walking until you have used all of the senses in creative ways.

There are other ways to develop the senses. Put a half dozen objects into a large cloth bag and give them to your child to see if he can figure out what they are by simply *feeling* the shape through the bag. Or, blindfold your child and give him some unusual textures to feel and try to identify: a woolly sweater, sandpaper, a file, and so on. You can do the same thing to develop the sense of taste. Blindfold your child and let him *taste* various foods. Mix up some that are familiar with some that are not.

S Is for Spelling Out Your Admiration

Spell out your admiration for each person in your family by writing his or her name in an acrostic fashion on a piece of paper and forming words from each letter that describe character qualities of that person. For example, the name Peter might work out this way:

P ATIENT
E NTHUSIASTIC
T EACHABLE
E NTERTAINING
R ESPONSIBLE

A good time to do this is on a birthday or on some other special day honoring that person, such as graduation day. Or, stage a Mutual Admiration Night when each member of the family honors the others. Tape or pin each person's acrostic to his bedroom door. It's a nice way of affirming one another in a tangible way.*

T Is for Tolerant

Be firm and tenacious, but always be tolerant. Yes, Dad, I know it's true that anything worth doing is worth doing well. But I also want to remember that my kids aren't robots. They are real, live human beings, and therefore prone to error.

Possibly the greatest obstacle to growth in our society is the *fear of failure.* One powerful way to help your children overcome that fear is to always let them feel the freedom to fail at home, in the family circle. Some questions I always ask myself include:

1. Am I willing to try new things myself and to fail in front of my kids on occasion?
2. When my children fail, am I tolerant or am I judgmental and impatient?
3. Do I take frequent opportunities to teach my children that mistakes are simply part of learning and growing?

What Kids Need Most in a Dad

I want my kids to grow up with high standards and good character qualities, but I don't want them to live in constant fear of failure. Home is the most important place for helping them discover that failure is not the end but only a stepping-stone to success.

Thomas Edison, the great inventor, was said to have "failed" thousands of times before he finally figured out the proper combination to make a successful light bulb. He would insist, however, that they were not failures or mistakes, simply "good education."

U Is for Unfinished

I frequently pass a store that has a big sign in the window: UNFINISHED FURNITURE. Each time I see a sign like that I'm reminded of the fact that that is exactly what we are in God's eyes. And, in some ways, we will always remain so.

One of the great reliefs to me as a dad is to know that I will always be unfinished. I will always be in process. I will never arrive (Philippians 3:13). You may be familiar with the button or sign with the letters PBPGINFWMY. This stands for, "Please Be Patient, God Is Not Finished With Me Yet." It's a great thought to keep in mind, not only for our children but also for ourselves. Have patience. There is no such thing as a finished product when it comes to being a dad—or a child. All of us are always learning. All of us are always growing.

It might be fun to make PBPGINFWMY buttons for all your family members and wear them on occasion. Talk about how we are always growing and learning more about what God wants us to be.

U Is for Utilize

I'm thinking especially of utilizing the many small chunks of time that all of us have. It's amazing what can be done in the ten minutes before dinner, or the twenty-five minutes during dinner, or the fifteen minutes after dinner.

My kids and I, for example, are trying to learn how to juggle. This is a great area where they can see me fail and have a good laugh about it at the same time. Ten minutes a day over a few weeks can accomplish miracles, however, whether it's in juggling or some other skill. I'm interested, for example, in encouraging my youngest son in his new reading skills. Taking ten minutes after dinner to practice reading can not only be a nice period of transition but it also gives him a great deal of encouragement in a skill that is going to be vital in his future.

During dinner, any number of things can happen. I know of one dad who insists that his children share at dinner each night one thing they have learned that day. If they can't come up with something, he keeps a dictionary handy and has them look up a word they have never seen before and share it with the family.

Likewise, dinner can be a wonderful time for practicing the almost lost art of asking good questions (*see* page 143). Help your children develop the art of conversation, the skills of listening and learning what really good questions sound like. Dinner can also be a time of planning the next outing, vacation, or other family project.

The possibilities are endless. The key is to use the moments while they are available. Don't wait until you "have time." You already do—if you will only utilize it!

V **Is for Values**

What are the six most important values that you want your children to have for life? Have you ever identified them specifically? If you have never identified those values, how can you know if you are teaching them?

For example, if honesty is important in your home, how are you teaching it? If trust is an important value to you, how are you utilizing daily opportunities to teach trust? If you want your kids to be responsible decision makers, what are you doing to help them discover how to make good decisions and accept the consequences of those decisions?

Values just don't happen. They must be learned and lived.

There's a story of a minister who got on the bus one day to travel across town. The bus driver gave him too much change. The minister didn't realize it until he was in his seat. As he recounted his change, he realized there was an oversight. As he got off the bus, he said to the driver, "I think there was some mistake. You gave me too much change." The bus driver replied, "Oh, no, sir, it was no mistake. I was in church on Sunday and I heard you preach about honesty. I just wanted to know if it was real in your life."

How would you set up a situation to help your children understand honesty? How do you model it in your own home? What are the specific ingredients of honesty? Do you realize, for example, that the word *integrity* (which is synonymous with *honesty*) also means "wholeness"? If your children cannot learn to be honest in little things, they will struggle in learning to be honest in the big things. If you want to know more about teaching your children values, try reading the following book: *Values and Faith,* by Roland Larson and Doris Larson, Winston Press, Inc., 1976, Minneapolis, Minnesota 55403.

W Is for Watching

One of the most strategic things you can do is to simply watch your children to understand their uniqueness as human beings. Proverbs 22:6 is translated, "Train a child in the way he should go, and when he is old he will not turn from it" (NIV). The more correct interpretation of the Hebrew, however, is, "Train up a child in his own way." In other words, train a child according to the way God made him or her, according to the child's particular temperament, abilities, and interests. Help your child understand that he or she is a one-of-a-kind human being and how to best use his or her life to honor God in a unique way.

In order to train your child in this fashion you need to watch and observe your child to see what he or she is like. The following are some questions you can ask yourself about your children as you set about your very important task of watching.

1. Do your children prefer to work alone or be with other people most of the time?
2. Do they tend to work best in a very structured environment or one that is more fluid?
3. Do they tend to enjoy mechanical "hands on" types of problems or more creative and artistic types of problems?
4. What is their favorite subject or subjects?
5. What are some of the things that seem to bother them the most? Likewise, what are some of the things that give them the most joy, happiness, and enthusiasm?
6. Do they tend to do one project at a time or do they like to be involved with several things at once?
7. What are their strengths and weaknesses?

8. What are their greatest skills and areas of inconsistency?
9. What are their favorite possessions?
10. What are their favorite hobbies?
11. Do they tend to make decisions more from their heads or more from their hearts?

The more carefully you watch your children, the better you will understand them. And as you understand them better, you will be able to help them understand themselves. To understand yourself is to be able to live in consistency with your own uniqueness. To paraphrase Proverbs 22:6, "Watch and train your child in his own way, according to how God made him or her, and it will be of lasting benefit through all of life."

W Is for Wild Idea

Surprise your youngster just before bedtime tonight with an invitation to sleep out in the backyard with you. Haul out the pads, sleeping bags, pillows, and snacks you've prepared, and head on out there. This kind of wild idea will put a little sparkle in your relationship. What you chat about while dozing off may be the freshest and most meaningful conversation you have had in quite a while.*

W Is for Wrestle

I once was interviewed by someone who asked me, "What is the most profound thing you do with your children?"

"Wrestle," I responded.

"No, you didn't quite understand," my interrogator said. "What do you do with your children that is really profound and meaningful?"

"Wrestle with them," I repeated. And then I went on to

explain that I really believe I can do no more profound act than to wrestle with my kids as often as possible. They love it and so do I. Am I trying to teach them to pursue a career in the ring? Hardly. When I wrestle with them I get to touch them, hug them, and occasionally even sneak in a kiss or two. Wrestling is a great way to love one another, and I highly recommend it for all dads.

X Is for Xenophobia

According to Webster's Dictionary, *xenophobia* is "the fear of strangers." Without apology, I suggest that you give your children (especially your younger ones) a mild dose of xenophobia with regard to strangers. In recent years, the horrible problem of child snatching has become acute. While you do not want to teach your children irrational fear, you do want to teach them to have a healthy respect for the family's rules on "stranger danger."

Talk with your children about what to do when they are approached by strangers, particularly strangers in cars who say they need to know the directions to some place, or who might even drive up saying, "Your mommy has been hurt and I'm supposed to take you to her." Have a clear understanding with your children about these matters. For example, if Mom or Dad were hurt, they would never send a stranger with the news.

Work out your own set of rules for dealing with strangers. Some of these would include:

1. When approached by a stranger on the street, keep right on going. Don't stop to engage in any conversations.
2. If a stranger drives up in a car and wants you to get in, keep moving. If the stranger follows along after you, run!

What Kids Need Most in a Dad

3. It's up to us as parents to be very clear and precise with our instructions. Have some prearranged places to run to for safety. In many communities, certain homes are labeled with special signs which tell children that home is a safe place to go if they are bothered by strangers.
4. Always emphasize to your children that they can certainly trust strangers *when they have been properly introduced* to these people by their parents, aunts or uncles, and other trusted people.

To repeat, you don't want your children to ever get a *serious* case of xenophobia. But a mild inoculation when they are small might save them from something far worse.

X Is for X Factor

The definition I like to use for *X Factor* is that "unknown quality or power that helps someone succeed or be effective." We once had a female instructor in our Summit Expedition program who was tremendously successful with every group she led. We tried to figure out her secret of success. She wasn't particularly outstanding in any way. She had no special gifts or abilities. Her personality was rather average. But then we hit on it. Her X Factor was her ability to listen. She really listened to her students and they responded to her in incredible ways.

What is your X Factor with your children? Maybe you can say, like the young woman I've just described, you are a good listener. Maybe it is your ability to talk, be amusing, or to be a confident leader.

If you can't think of an X Factor, may I suggest one that applies to everybody? The X Factor that all of us need is prayer. Every father can be a man of prayer. Indeed, many fathers have told me that they weren't men of prayer until they became fathers! We say it so often that it's become a cliché, but there is no truer statement: "As a dad I need to pray for my kids—without ceasing."

Y Is for Yes

A little earlier I talked about why *no* is one of the best words ever invented for dads. *Yes* is also a good word, but for different reasons. I may need to learn how to say no to my kids at times, but I need to learn how to say yes to my family.

I need to learn how to say, "Yes, I have time for you." "Yes, I care." "Yes, I'll listen long and hard, even though sometimes I don't understand."

I need to say, "Yes, I'll pray about that," and keep my word. I need to learn how to say yes to my wife more often when she wants to tell me about her day. I need to say yes to my kids when they ask me if I want to go out and play a little bit.

I want to be a dad who says yes when my kids say, "Can we talk, Dad?" Or, "Dad, do you still love me even when I don't do so well?"

Yes is a marvelous word. True, I can't always say yes to everything. I may not be able to say yes when my teenager wants the car. I may not be able to say yes when my children want to do something that I know is not right or safe. But I hope I can always say yes when it comes to giving my life each and every day for my family. In 2 Corinthians 4 Paul writes a beautiful paragraph about doing just that. He says:

> *We are hard-pressed on all sides, but we are never frustrated; we are puzzled, but never in despair. We are persecuted, but are never deserted: we may be knocked down but we are never knocked out! Every*

What Kids Need Most in a Dad

day we experience something of the death of Jesus, so that we may also show the power of the life of Jesus in these bodies of ours. Yes, we who are living are always being exposed to death for Jesus' sake, so that the life of Jesus may be plainly seen in our mortal lives.

2 Corinthians 4:8–11 PHILLIPS

Z Is for Zachary

By the time you get to the end of the alphabet, you might expect it would be difficult to come up with things beginning with Z. In this case, however, I've saved one of the best for the last letter of the alphabet. Z is for Zachary, the number-one reason I'm a father. Zac, you see, is my first son. His name means "he who God remembers." He is nine years old right now—sensitive, curious, gentle. He is a young, fresh, wonderful human being who never ceases to surprise or amaze me. He is one of the two very particular reasons that I'm a dad and the reason being a father is more than just a good idea to me.

Zac is different from his brother, Josh, but I don't do as much comparing of the two as I do admiring their special interests and gifts. These days Zac is into swimming and he says someday he might be in the Olympics. I wouldn't put it past him. I'm grateful he can dream big dreams, and I hope he never loses that quality.

Zac is no prodigy but he's no slouch, either. One evening as we were driving down to the pizza shop, he said to me as he looked at the moon, "Hey, Dad, is the moon going toward full or quarter?"

I hadn't even noticed and had to admit I didn't know. Zac said, "I think it's going toward full. I've been watching it the last few nights."

Then Zac asked, "Hey, Pop, how does that eclipse thing work again?"

I said to him, "That's a little complicated . . ." but I went ahead and gave it to him anyway. I explained to Zac that an eclipse happens when the earth gets between the sun and the moon and blocks out the sun's reflection.

"Oh, yeah," Zac said. And then he decided to help his little brother, Josh, understand it, too.

Zac pulled down the visor over the front seat of the car so that the mirror would catch the headlights of the car behind us and reflect them on the ceiling. He then explained to Josh that the moon gets its light by being reflected from the sun. Then Zac stuck his hand between the mirror and the roof of the car to block off the light.

"This is what Dad means by an eclipse, Josh. Do you see what I mean?"

I was amazed by Zac's quick and practical illustration of an eclipse to his six-year-old brother. Frankly, he did it better than I ever could.

It's fun being Zac's dad. My prayer is that I can grow up along with him and not get in the way of, or hamper, his natural intelligence. I'm sure you can see why I close this Alphabet of Fathering with Z—for Zac. Thanks for the privilege of being your dad, son.

Chapter Eight Notes

1. Cindy Herbert and Susan Russell, *Everychild's Everyday* (Garden City, New York: Doubleday & Co., Inc., 1980).

2. Quoted by Leo Buscaglia in *Love* (New York: Fawcett Book Group, 1982), p. 52.

3. Erwin Lutzer, *If I Could Change My Mom and Dad* (Chappaqua, New York: Christian Herald, 1982), p. 75.

4. Roy Lessin, *How to Be Parents of Happy and Obedient Children* (Medford, Oregon: Omega Publications, 1978), p. 92.

5. Address for Dad's Only is P.O. Box 340, Julian, California 92036.

What Kids Need Most in a Dad

Nine
The Prime Essentials of Fathering: Time, Consistency, and Enthusiasm
But the Greatest of These Is Enthusiasm

The essential sadness of our human family is that very few of us even approach the realization of our full potential. I accept the estimate of the theoreticians that the average person accomplishes only 10 percent of his promise. He sees only 10 percent of the beauty in the world about him. He hears only 10 percent of the music and poetry in the universe. He smells only a tenth of the world's fragrance, and tastes only a tenth of the deliciousness of being alive. He is only 10 percent open to his emotions, to tenderness, to wonder and awe. His mind embraces only a small part of the thoughts, reflections and understanding of which he is capable. His heart is only 10 percent alive with love. He will die without ever having really lived or really loved. To me, this is the most frightening of all possibilities. I would really hate

to think that you or I might die without having really lived and really loved.

John Powell[1]

Maturity: among other things—not to hide one's strength out of fear and, consequently, live below one's best. . . . Not I, but God in me. . . . I am the vessel, the draught is God's—and God is the thirsty One. . . . Without looking back—to say YES!

Dag Hammarskjold[2]

A father is someone who spends time with you and takes you on vacation and talks to you about the world and life in general. A father is someone who has fun with you. A father is loyal. A father is honest. A father is trustworthy. A father is a leader. A father is love. A father is someone who goes through a lot of pain and sorrow, but he is still a father. A father is not someone who runs away from life. He is there to cope and work things out. A father is not a coward. A father is love.

Mary, Teenage Girl

Recently I was asked, "In all the complexities of fathering, what are the essentials?"

That's a very good and a very tough question, and I can only answer for myself. In my opinion, the prime essentials of fathering are: time, consistency, and passionate enthusiasm. These three are my ultimate X Factors in fathering. Without these, I cannot do a quality job.

The Myth of "Quality Time"

If I want to be a quality dad I have to spend the time. But please don't confuse being a quality dad with spending "quality time" with your kids. The term *quality time* has become so abused and overused that we begin to think we can give our kids just little moments of time here and there as long as they are "quality." The only problem with that statement is reality. My kids don't know the difference between regular time and quality time. They don't make such silly divisions. They simply value me and the time that I can spend with them. I believe that when we start using terms and images such as *quality time* we begin to devalue the intrinsic wonder of life itself.

Life is time-consuming. Time is the very crucible of fathering. The most profound way I let my family know I love them is by giving them time. Of course I want that time to have elements of quality in it. I want it to be properly planned. I want it to have clarity and creativity, but at the bottom line there is no substitute for the wonder of time itself. Time is the platform on which life is built, the very track on which we all run. Time is the path between us and our children.

How does your use of time match up with your values and priorities? Each year I try to answer that question for myself. On the left side of the page I write down all my priorities. On the right-hand side I try to list, as best I can, how I use my time. I'm always shocked to see that sometimes the left- and right-hand columns are in inverse proportion. In other words, what I say I value most is actually that to which I commit the least time. The urgent and the necessary always seem to creep in and edge out the important and the vital.

In *When I Relax I Feel Guilty,* I use the illustration of how at age thirty-five you have only five hundred days left to live. My thesis is that if you live until age seventy or seventy-one, in the next thirty-five or thirty-six years you will have to spend a great deal of your time sleeping, working, eating, and traveling. You will also have to tend to personal matters such as hygiene and maintaining good health. There will be the odd chores and the myriad of miscellaneous time stealers that often come in the form of "emergencies." My estimate is that in the next thirty-five or thirty-six years, after taking care of all of the "necessary" things, you will have roughly the equivalent of five hundred days to spend as you wish.[3]

When I put life in that context, it helps me realize that I

am a father for so short a time. I dare not take it for granted. If I want to be the very best possible father I can be, I cannot do it without the essential commitment of my time.

Time to Stop, Look, Listen

Joshua, my six-year-old, was practicing his reading with me the other day. The book was entitled *Stop, Look, Listen.* I realized that was valuable advice.

As a dad, the first thing I've always got to do is take time to stop—to pray, to be, to just hug and hold my kids, to truly enjoy being a father. I have some very dear friends who almost lost their home recently in one of those famous California brush fires. The flames were so close they were licking over the patio and roof. My friends were out of town at the time and only the heroic efforts of neighbors saved the day. Some wet down the roof while others quickly moved furniture and other personal items out into the yard just in case the house did go.

I talked to Peg and Gary after they returned and she said, "Oh, it's such a *wonderful mess!*" She realized it would be weeks before she could clean up the soot and ashes and get things back together, but she still knew that it was wonderful to have the mess to clean up, rather than have nothing but ashes.

I can't help comparing the experience of Peg and Gary with being a father. There are plenty of brush fires, but the question for me is, do I stop and realize what a wonderful mess my home and family can be?

In chapter 4, I challenged all of us to take time to see our kids for real. To take time to stop and look means that we're close enough to our kids to be available. It means really seeing them for who they are in the midst of their dreams, hopes, and frustrations.

What my kids seem to want more than anything else is my attention. They go through antic after antic to try and get

What Kids Need Most in a Dad

me to stop and look. Some days the best thing I can do for them is sit on the back porch and watch them ride their bikes over the little ramp they've built. Or, I can take a look at the work that they've brought home from school.

It's been said that love is blind. I'm beginning to see that the opposite is really true. Our love opens our eyes to take time to see the miracles of change going on in our children right before our eyes. We can be victims of various kinds of blindness, but one of the most tragic would be family blindness—not really seeing those we love and with whom we live.

The Most Important Need of All

While blindness can be tragic, deafness can be worse. If there's anything we must do as we stop to look it is to also listen.

As Paul Tournier said so well:

> *It is impossible to overemphasize the immense need humans have to be really listened to, to be taken seriously, to be understood. No one can develop freely in this world and find the life full without feeling understood by at least one person. . . . Listen to all the conversations of our world, between nations as well as those between couples, they are, for the most part, dialogues of the deaf.*[4]

The proof of Tournier's statement is seen in the many listening seminars that are conducted by specialists throughout the country and around the world. A few years ago I attended one such seminar. Conducted by Lyman K. Steil, it opened my eyes and ears to the immensity of the problem of lack of listening. Professor Steil, who heads up his own firm, Communications Consultants Associated, pointed out that we spend 80 percent of our waking hours

What Kids Need Most in a Dad   167

trying to communicate with one another. About 45 percent of that time is spent listening. But what does our educational system teach us to do? It spends most of its time trying to teach us how to write, which we use only 9 percent of the time, and how to read, which we use only 10 percent of the time. If we are lucky we are also given some courses in how to speak, which we use 30 percent of the time. But rarely, if ever, are people taught to be good listeners, something they have to do 45 percent of the time![5]

So, we grow up not learning how to listen. We marry and have children and we pass on our lack of listening skills to them. It is no wonder that parents and children often complain of having nothing in common or of not being able to understand one another. The word *communication* comes from *communus,* a Latin root meaning "having something in common." Perhaps the so-called generation gap is really a communication gap. If we are to close that gap we have to start listening to one another. I don't know of anyone who could lead the way better than a servant father who is dedicated to improving his listening skills. There's no better way to demonstrate our love for our mates and our children.

Every day we listen to messages written on the wind, so to speak. Once said, they are gone. Are we really hearing them? The cost of poor listening in the family is difficult to measure. But it is safe to say that lack of listening will affect your child's self-esteem, his human effectiveness, his hopes and dreams, his ability to think clearly, his attitudes and values.

You Can Learn to Listen Better

Fortunately, listening is a learned behavior, and we can all learn to do it much better than we have before. During Dr. Steil's seminar I learned about four levels of listening that are synonymous with the four purposes of communication. The four levels are diagramed below. Dr. Steil emphasizes that these four levels are like a triangle with each level built upon the other. How we communicate at the higher levels is largely influenced by how well we communicate at the lower ones.[6]

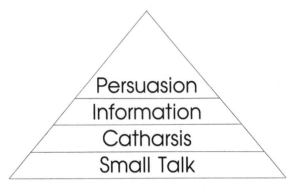

The first level is phatic communication, or in simpler terms, "small talk." Phatic means "to bind people together," and that's exactly what small talk does. We need a lot of small talk with our kids—conversations about school, friends, their hopes and their dreams. Small talk is not a waste of time. It is your basis for building a personal relationship with your child.

The second level is cathartic communication, where pent-up emotions are released. It is probably the most important level for our children to use while going through the frustrating process of growing up. For cathartic communication to occur, your child must be able to vent his feelings and frustrations while you listen to them carefully. And there also has to be a solid base of that small talk, which leads to the second level where your child can share his feelings, his fears, his joys, in short, his emotions. I believe there is little doubt that cathartic communication is the key level where we dads must listen much more carefully.

The third level is informative communication, that of sharing ideas, information, or data. A problem for a lot of us dads is that we are too interested in communicating at this level, but we don't take time to communicate at the small talk and cathartic levels first. We tend to be too interested in making sure everybody understands the situation, the facts, the numbers, the right time to be there, and so on. But if we want our children to be better listeners at the information level, let's be sure that we do two things: (1) listen at the two levels below (cathartic and small talk); and (2) listen carefully to the information our family sends our way.

The fourth level is persuasive communication, in which we try to get others to do what we want or see things our way. Ironically, it is at this level that parents want to spend most of their time and effort. After all, the Scriptures tell us the purpose of parenting is to "train up our children" (*see* Proverbs 22:6) and to "bring them up in the nurture and admonition of the Lord" (*see* Ephesians 6:4).

We believe, and rightly so, that our job as parents is to help our children learn how to behave, how to have good attitudes, how to get along with others. But the problem in most homes is that the parents think the children are irresponsible, bratty, not willing to listen, while the children think the parents are ogres, bossy, unreasonable, and "always lecturing." When you look at the situation through the diagram of the four levels of communication, the problem becomes much easier to understand. The reason parents don't communicate as well as they like at the persuasion level is that they haven't spent enough time at the three levels below. We are busy trying to correct our children when we haven't taken the time to use small talk, catharsis, and the sharing of information.

As Dr. Steil emphasizes again and again in his seminars, if two people are at different levels, communication is difficult, or it does not take place at all. If we want to influence and persuade our children, we must:

1. Become better listeners.
2. Learn how to communicate with our children on the level where they are at the moment.
3. Learn how to communicate at lower levels—especially small talk and feelings—before moving on to the higher levels of information sharing and persuasion.

Admittedly, this is not simple. It takes time and patience. But there is probably no more crucial way to spend your time with your children than in learning how to communicate with them more effectively. So, stop, look, and listen, Dad. Persevere and be willing to fail and to be frustrated. It may be more complicated than you thought it would be, but that simply makes it more exciting.

The Secret to Consistency

My second prime essential for fathering is consistency. The best definition I know of for *consistency* is "perseverance that is in balance." We persevere at something we love to do. We persist at something that we deeply care about. In the long run, dads who are successful hang in there in spite of the setbacks. They remain consistent to who they are and what they know to be true.

Each of us has his own unique design and pattern as a human being. Each of us has his own unique relationship with Jesus Christ. Who we are and what we believe will be reflected in our family as each of us works out his own unique style of fathering.

The key to being consistent is finding out who I am and what my particular style of fathering is. I know that no matter how poor a job I do at being Tim Hansel, nobody can do that job better than I can. As I go about the task of being me, I find my own unique style and instead of worrying about my mistakes, I learn from them as I build on my strengths and personal commitment to God and my family.

Five Steps to Becoming

Finding our own style and particular strengths is not easy. When I taught psychology at the high school level I developed a course that focused on five major points I believe are essential in the process of becoming who we are. These five points are just as relevant to fathers as they were to my high school students. In fact, as a father learns these five points, he could then pass them on to his own children.

1. *Accept Yourself.* At some time, each of us has to confront his own uniqueness and embrace it without apology, without excuse, and without complaint. The process of becoming cannot begin until we truly accept ourselves as original creations. I am a one-of-a-kind human being and a one-of-a-kind father.

People often ask me, "Well, how is this accepting done?" I in turn ask them how they accepted Jesus Christ into their lives. They usually answer that at some point they simply had enough information and desire to invite Christ into their lives. I point out that the self-acceptance process is very similar. At some point each of us must make a decision and say, "From now on I do, in fact, accept who I am." Self-acceptance is a necessary (and wonderful) beginning of a long journey of self-discovery.

2. *Know Yourself.* As we accept ourselves we can begin to know who we truly are. A senior in my psychology class once said to me, "I've gone to school all my life, and I probably will go some more, but I hope I will never have to say in the end that I know a subject better than I know myself."

Knowing yourself means getting in touch with the special gifts God has given you. Each of us has strengths and weaknesses as a father. Have you stopped long enough to identify them? As I know my weaknesses I know what I need to work on and what to watch out for. As I know my strengths I know what I should be doing and where I am going. As I know myself I unlock the incredible potential God has put within me.

3. *Be Yourself.* Once we have accepted ourselves and know something about our gifts, the next task is to share those gifts in our family with enthusiastic abandon. This sharing or releasing of our gifts is not as easy as it may seem. If you are like me, at times you can identify with the servant in the parable of the talents who said, "I was afraid and went out and hid your talent in the ground . . ." (Matthew 25:25 NIV).

Many of us know how this servant felt. Even in our own family circle we sometimes fear we will be rejected. So, we repress our gifts and bury our talents. We withhold the very miracle that is us. Being and using yourself is costly. Being the best father you know how requires risk. You can become so dependent upon the approval of others, including the approval of those in your family, that you tend to mold your personality around the pervasive goal of gaining their full approval all of the time.

There's a lot of talk today about headship and how the man is to be leader in his home. Without getting into involved debates about the meaning of *headship* and *submission,* we can simply go about being who we are and doing what is necessary. You are the leader, Dad, so get on with it. Don't try to imitate the Super Dad stereotypes you've heard about. Do what you believe a servant father should be doing in that situation. Sometimes everyone will approve; on other occasions you may have to call some shots your wife or children don't like. Call them anyway, not because you just want to "do your own thing and everybody had better listen up," but because of your love and concern. To be sure, you may make mistakes, but always re-

What Kids Need Most in a Dad   173

member that the Super Dads who never make mistakes are myths. Servant fathers who try to be themselves are very real.

4. *Love Yourself.* Some people think that loving yourself is a strange inclusion in the five-step sequence. It is, however, essential. Not until we can truly love ourselves can we move on to the ultimate place where we abandon ourselves in Christ and know the secret to the great paradox of losing our lives in order to find them.

But what does it mean to love myself? Self-love is no ill-disguised form of vanity. When Jesus gave the two great commandments, He told us to love God with all our heart, soul, mind, and strength, and to love our neighbor *as ourselves* (Matthew 22:34–40). Surely our closest "neighbors" are those in our family. We can only love them in direct proportion to how much we love ourselves. But Jesus isn't inviting us to a narcissistic orgy. Loving myself is based on self-acceptance, self-knowledge, and being myself. When I finally realize that Jesus has come to set me free to love myself, then I am free indeed. I am free from the penalty of sin and from its all pervading power. I am free from the constant need to prove myself, to justify myself. I don't have to be afraid because Christ's perfect love has driven out the fear and I can move on to the final and most important step.

5. *Forget Yourself.* One of Jesus Christ's most radical promises is that if I lose my life for His sake, I will truly find it (Matthew 16:24–26). Those can be puzzling words until we understand that we cannot lose ourselves until we find ourselves. One of the greatest problems in the church today is that we keep talking about losing our lives before we even know who we are and before we get in touch with what it means to accept ourselves, know ourselves, be ourselves, and love ourselves. Obviously, it is a sequence that

What Kids Need Most in a Dad

we cannot do "once and for all." It is a constant challenge, and as Jesus said, we must take up our cross daily and follow Him.

And as we take up that cross we actually do forget ourselves. We become more concerned about the will of God than our own reputation. We become more concerned about the lives of those wonderful people in our family than we are about ourselves. It means that we become secure enough to be real, and real enough to go beyond our own security to meet the needs around us. It means that we begin to discover the power in being fully human and fully alive.

Above all, it means that we can become like the servant father I have tried to describe throughout this book. We can face and meet the challenge of crucifying our own desires in order to be free in Christ to be the best kind of father possible with a sense of abandonment, dedication, and passion.

I hope you begin to see and feel with me why consistency is such a prime essential in fathering. As I said, consistency is a balanced kind of perseverance. It is a blend of courage, patience, and my own unique style, all of which I apply daily in my home. Because I am a one-of-a-kind father, I am free to be real—to be the very best father I can be. As my personality is set free in Christ, I can become a true servant leader in my own home. I can discover the eternal continuity of life that goes beyond puny comparisons and man-made standards. I can become free to see and hear and touch my children with a sense of saving wonder.

And the Greatest of These Is Enthusiasm

We have looked at the prime essentials of time and consistency, and now we come to the greatest and most elusive one of all: enthusiasm. And this all-important prime essential *is* elusive, even for the most enthusiastic and passionate father. Boredom and apathy have become communicable diseases that infect our future-shocked society. We all know men who have already "retired" at the age of thirty-five but are just staying on the job for another thirty years or so. I know many fathers who in a sense "retired" from fathering long ago. They have ceased trying new ideas. They have ceased being creative. Their passion for fathering has long since faded. Suffocated by frustrations, disappointments, and bewilderment they have donned a mere "costume," and in it they play the part of a dad, but they are just going through the motions. They rationalize their condition by observing that a lot of other fathers seem to be in the same boat, or they simply repress the problem and assume that no one else could know or understand the pain of their complicated situation.

The Handy-Dandy Excuse List

Is there a way for a dad to know if he is ailing from these diseases of boredom and apathy? Is there a way to know if you are starting to get infected?

One day as I was having a cup of coffee I played around with what I call the "Handy-Dandy Excuse List for Dads." The way to use this list is to think about all of your challenges, responsibilities, and involvements as a father. As you think about all these, check the boxes that seem appropriate to the situations.

1. _____ Don't have time.
2. _____ Don't have time.
3. _____ Don't have time.
4. _____ Never trained.
5. _____ Don't know what to do.
6. _____ I don't care.

What Kids Need Most in a Dad

You'll note that the first three lines are all the same: "Don't have time." My reason for this is that it's the most common excuse we give for our failures to do what we should. To say I don't have time is an easy way out. To say I don't have time is typical but not necessarily serious. I can change all that by simply making time. We all do what we really want to do. Time is relative. If we want to make time for something, we can.

Other excuses such as "No training" or "Don't know how" are sometimes valid, but they, too, can be corrected. The most dangerous line in my little Handy-Dandy Excuse List is obviously the last one. If I check "I don't care," the ball game is over. Once the enthusiasm for fathering has dissolved, everything else begins to erode and slip away. My impotency stifles all of my family relationships, and my excuses for my boredom and apathy begin to abound from all sides.

So, the obvious question is, how do we avoid checking that box labeled "I don't care"? I am reminded of two passages of Scripture: In John's Revelation he is instructed to write to the church at Ephesus and tell them, "You have forsaken your first love. Remember the height from which you have fallen! Repent and do the things you did at first . . ." (Revelation 2:4, 5 NIV).

And in I Peter 4:8 we are reminded that love can cover a multitude of sins.

If boredom and apathy are setting in, Dad, maybe the first thing you need to do is pray. It is significant that the word *enthusiasm* comes from the Greek root *entheos,* which means, "God dwells within us." As we saw in the section on consistency, real *entheos* occurs as we learn to forget ourselves and lose our lives in Christ, in order to save them. It is hard to be complacent about fathering (or anything else) if we have given up our rights to take up His cross and follow Him.

What Kids Need Most in a Dad   177

The tragedy is, some of us have grown accustomed to our complacency. On the back of one of my worn New Testaments it says there are three ways to avoid criticism: say nothing, do nothing, be nothing. Sadly enough, this can happen to fathers who have given up on the promises of Scripture. Because they lack the time or the training or the know-how, they console themselves with the thought that as long as they do nothing, they won't make any mistakes.

I want to say in as many ways as I can that the greatest mistake a father can make is to not love his family with a passion that is uncompromising, enduring, and unfailing. A father needs the patient endurance that struggles through the winters of life. A father needs the wisdom of the often-quoted proverb to not curse the darkness but to light one small candle.

A father needs to hold fast to his dream and to continue to believe that God does keep His promises. A father needs courage to bear what seems unbearable. Like anyone who has wrestled with God, he may be wounded in the thigh, but he limps back into the thick of the battle with a renewed confidence. A father needs meekness, which may be accurately described as strong passion under control.

I don't believe fathers are called to always be in complete control of the situation. We are called to act, to love, and to suffer if necessary, and through all this we conquer because of who Jesus was and is: the living Christ.

A father needs to play to win. I'll never forget the words of Ray Meyer, the famed basketball coach of DePaul University, whose team lost an important semifinal game in the NCAA Tournament. Asked what the problem was he commented, "Our greatest error was that we played 'not to lose' instead of *playing to win.*"

If I'm going to be the kind of father who really makes a difference in my children's lives, I must play to win. And the first step in playing to win is accepting my full responsibility as the leader of my home and committing myself to the prime essentials of time, consistency, and enthusiasm.

Friedrich Hegel, one of history's greatest philosophers, spent much of his life thinking. Yet Hegel is the one who said, "We may affirm absolutely that *nothing* great in the world has been accomplished without passion."[7]

So, play to win, Dad. Never play "not to lose." Play to *win.* The stakes are high, the wounds sometimes deep and painful, but the prize is more than worth it. Elbert Hubbard said it so well. In the end, "God will not look you over for medals, degrees or diplomas but for scars."[8]

Chapter Nine Notes

1. John Powell, *The Secret of Staying in Love* (Allen, Texas: Argus Communications, 1974), p. 11.

2. Dag Hammarskjold, *Markings* (New York: Alfred A. Knopf, Inc., 1964), pp. 89–91.

3. Tim Hansel, *When I Relax I Feel Guilty* (Elgin, Illinois: David C. Cook Publishing Co., 1979), p. 67.

4. Paul Tournier, *To Understand Each Other* (Atlanta: John Knox Press, 1967), p. 8.

5. *See* Lyman K. Steil, "Secrets of Being a Better Listener," *U.S. News and World Report,* May 26, 1980.

6. For additional material on the four levels of communication, *see* Salvatore A. Conigliaro, "Listen Your Way to the Top," *Graduating Engineer* (Winter 1980), pp. 15–17.

7. George Seldes, compiler, *The Great Quotations* (Secaucus, New Jersey: Lyle Stuart, Inc., 1966), p. 715.

8. Elbert Hubbard, quoted in *Laurels for Father* (Norwalk, Connecticut: C.R. Gibson Co., 1968).

Epilogue
And Afterward . . .
A Tribute (of Sorts) to My Dad

I call this epilogue a "tribute of sorts" for two reasons:

- I can't end a book on fathering without saying something special about my own father. Call it a salute, a king-size compliment—he deserves one more word of recognition.
- I'm not sure whether I want to salute my dad or thank him. Each year I discover more of the power in gratitude. Some consider it the heart of all other virtues because it gives the others their strength and value. There may be some truth in that. Significantly enough, thanksgiving is the only virtue we celebrate with its own holiday.

There is so much I am thankful for. I'm sure I would have difficulty placing priorities on all of it: the wonder of a handshake . . . a note from a friend . . . my son simply saying, "Hi, Dad" . . . a dog who has been a dear friend for over thirteen years.

What Kids Need Most in a Dad

This year in particular I'm learning again the blessings of brokenness and the unbelievable privilege of being made whole again. The greatness of God sneaks up on us in all these little daily events.

And this year more than any other in my life I have been overwhelmed by a deepening gratitude for having a family. This gratitude comes in a twofold sense. Never before have I been so aware of the privilege of *having* a dad—and *being* one as well. Never before have I realized the depth of the sacrifices my parents made for me over the years and how I've never been able to truly thank them for that. Never before have I been so stunned in realizing all my wife has held back in her own life in order to enhance mine. And never before have I realized so clearly that my children are a gift to enjoy for such a short time.

All of these "never befores" remind me of a favorite saying I picked up from the late Dag Hammarskjold, former secretary general of the United Nations: "If only I may grow: firmer, simpler—quieter, warmer."[1]

I have pondered Hammarskjold's words many times, always hoping that some day I might emerge as the kind of man my father always was. This book has not only been written *for* him but *because* of him, and the amazing woman he chose to spend his entire life with over four and a half decades ago.

My folks seem to be immersed in plain-brown-wrapper humanity. They are coated with deep, simple, unembroidered human decency. Their contentment is so quiet it almost goes unnoticed. Oh, they're not saints by any of the plastic definitions. They're not the kind you want to put up on the shelf in some kind of display. But they are the kind of people who haven't deferred life in search of something else.

My dad has never been much for the exterior stuff. At work and at home he is nothing but a man. We live in a society where thousands of people pay hundreds of dollars a week to "find out who they are," but my dad has always known who he is. Art Hansel. Nothing more. And certainly nothing less.

I wrote the following poem just after learning that my dad, now seventy-six, has cancer. I wrote it to honor this very special man whom I have the privilege of calling my father. In so many ways he is just another man, made in God's image, wearing a white shirt with a clip-on tie and a ready smile for all those people he calls "friend." You may have noticed this book is dedicated to him and to my brother, who served as my "other father" when my dad was busy working two jobs—which was most of his life.

Dad, you see, never gave up. My original choice for the title of this book was *Never, Never, Never Give Up.* Almost forty years ago my father gave me a wonderful little plaque that said simply: NEVER GIVE UP. Not surprisingly he proceeded to live out that simple motto before my eyes, and he's still doing it. The NEVER GIVE UP plaque still hangs above my desk and contains three of the most powerful and important words I've ever heard or read.

I cannot think of any better way to close this book than by combining the words on that plaque with the following poem. Although I could remember so much my dad *did,* when the words came they seemed to center on what he *didn't.* I hope "But You Didn't" will serve to remind you how special, and how temporary, the privilege of fatherhood is.

I got the inspiration for this poem about my father from another poem which was shared with me by one of my students some thirteen years ago. The same poem recently appeared in Leo Buscaglia's book *Living, Loving & Learning* (Thorofare, New Jersey: Charles B. Slack, Inc.), pp. 75, 76. The title of the original poem was "Things You Didn't Do."

BUT YOU DIDN'T

Dad,
   Remember when I broke the window at the neighbor's
      house?
   You know, the great big one?
      I tried to get you excited about the fact that I'd hit a
         home run
      in the process;
      But by the look on your face when you found out how
         much it was
      going to cost,
         I thought you were going to strangle me,
                    BUT YOU DIDN'T

And remember when you found out that I had sold the
   minister some books on how
   to mix drinks (that I'd found in the alley)
   just to make some extra money for Christmas presents?
I thought for sure that you were going to tell me that there
   was going to be
      no more Christmas for me,
                    BUT YOU DIDN'T

Do you remember, Dad, when I borrowed your best knife,
   kinda without your knowing it,
      and kinda lost it?
O I felt awful.
   I *knew* that you were going to tell me that I was a
      screwed-up, irresponsible kid,
                    BUT YOU DIDN'T

Remember, Dad,
   when I split my head open for the fourth time
      in only three years?
For sure, I expected you to tell me that it was a really dumb
   thing to do,
                    BUT YOU DIDN'T

What Kids Need Most in a Dad   183

O Dad,
    Can you remember when you tried to teach me how to
        drive?
    And I became an instant imbecile, unable to remember
        which pedal did what,
    making the car jump up and down all over the road?
I felt certain that you'd adopt me out to another family until
    I finally learned
    how to drive,
BUT YOU DIDN'T

And, can you remember, Dad,
    when you let me use your car, for that "extra special"
        date
    and I got into an accident because I was trying to show
        off?
I was afraid to come home because I told her you were
    going to ground me . . .
    for at least a year,
BUT YOU DIDN'T

O Dad,
    you were always surprising me, always loving me more
        than I ever deserved.
    Somehow you always knew just what I needed.
Like, remember when I didn't make the team that year and
    I came home in tears, feeling pretty sorry for myself?
I was confident that you'd join me in my self-pity party,
BUT YOU DIDN'T

Or, years later
    when I finally made the All City and All State teams
    and even got a scholarship to go to Stanford?
I thought you'd be so impressed and tell me that now I
    "really had life made,"
BUT YOU DIDN'T

                           What Kids Need Most in a Dad

I guess that's why you didn't seem so surprised when
I got thrown in jail for "celebrating a little bit too hard" after
   a State
Championship game.
Remember, Dad, (how could you ever forget)
   when you and Mom got a phone call at 4:30 in the
      morning from the
   chief of police asking you to come down to the jail and
      get your son?
All the way home I waited and waited for you to blast me,
               BUT YOU DIDN'T

The first words, in fact the only words, you said to me were:
   "Come on, *son,* let's go have some breakfast."
How did you know, Dad? How did you know?
   At the time of most critical failure; at the very time when
      I knew that
   I had let you down the most, you knew, you remembered
      to remind me that
      I was your *son*—period . . . in spite of it all.
         How did you know?
For a man with only an eighth-grade education and no
   time to read,
   because you were always working more than one job just
      to keep your family going,
   you were sure smart.
No, more than that, Dad, you had some of that "wisdom"
   that must have come
         from the Other Father.
You always told me that you and "The Man Upstairs" (as
   you were fond of calling Him)
   were pretty close friends.
The years passed,
   and our friendship grew even closer.
I can remember, Dad,

What Kids Need Most in a Dad   185

the first time we had lunch together—just you and me,
   alone.
I was in my late twenties—almost a grown man.
   We laughed and you told me stories about your youth
      that I never knew before.
   That lunch seemed to go on forever.
After that,
   you seemed even closer and I began to realize who you
      really were . . .
   and how much I really loved you.
Memories . . .
   Special ones . . .
      Aren't we fortunate, Dad,
         to have so many?
Steve and I have a lot of rich memories,
   because you made sure that we experienced a lot of life
      . . . together.
REMEMBER, DAD,
   when we used to go duck hunting and Midnight, our little
      dog, was so small
      that she couldn't drag the ducks back?
   when Steve got his first car?
   when I brought forty-three kids home from a Young Life
      camp at three in the morning,
      to sleep on the floor?
   when you and Mom could dance all night and still knock
      the socks off
      everybody at work the next day?
   when your sons finally graduated from college (it was
      something you always
      wanted for us)?
REMEMBER, DAD,
   when Steve, your number-one son and my number-one
      friend,
      got married in Boston?
   What a grand celebration. You were so proud.

What Kids Need Most in a Dad

when we couldn't wrestle anymore?
when you got honored for being the top man in your
   region—
    an honor few men get (still working) at the age of
     seventy-four?
when you first had to tell me that "California was a long
   ways away"
    and that you would like to come down, but maybe
     later . . . ?
O Dad,
   I've never quite had enough words to be able to tell you
    and Mom
    just how much I love you.
Remember when
   Pam and I finally got our first house
    and children came?
We wanted so much for you to be able to come visit,
             BUT YOU DIDN'T

You couldn't anymore.
   For a growing number of reasons.
You wanted to so much,
   but California was "such a long way."
Remember, Dad,
   the day they broke the news to you
    that you had cancer?
   Everyone else seemed to fall to pieces,
             BUT YOU DIDN'T

Never have I been more proud of you, Pop.
   The quiet courage that you showed us all those years,
    sometimes when we weren't even aware of it,
   has shown all the more brightly these past months.
I never heard you complain.
   In fact, I've never seen you laugh more richly, Pop,
    and never seen you so much at peace.

What Kids Need Most in a Dad   187

I'm understanding,
   at even deeper levels,
      those three precious words you gave me four decades
      ago:
              "Never Give Up."

           because . . . YOU DIDN'T!

As I mentioned, "But You Didn't" was written just after I learned that my dad has cancer. I never thought he would live long enough to see this book, dedicated to him, get into print. But he fooled me again. Although he has cancer of the lungs and the entire lymph system, he finished his last radiation treatment and chemotherapy a few months ago. We just celebrated his seventy-sixth birthday and this morning he told me on the phone he was "a little worn out" from walking all the way around the block.

Oh, yes, he's still working at his job, still shooting for "Man of the Year."

In fact, when he read "But You Didn't" he said he liked it a lot, but he wanted to remind me that he's not ready for memorials just yet. He's planning to stay around and be my father for a few more years. He's like that.

Thanks, Dad.

                    I love you,
                    Tim

Epilogue Notes

1. Dag Hammarskjold, *Markings* (New York: Alfred A. Knopf, Inc., 1964), p. 93.

Tim Hansel is president of Summit Expedition, a nonprofit California corporation providing adventure-based educational experiences for people of all ages and backgrounds. For more information about Summit Expedition write: P.O. Box 521, San Dimas, CA 91773, or call: (818) 915-3331.